THE LABYRINTH OF HEALING

OF HEALING

The Emotional Shifting Process

THE LABYRINTH
OF HEALING

ISBN - 9780692830604
Book design by Sean Keenan
Edited by Dreamwalker Publishing
Publisher: Dreamwalker Publishing LLC
www.dr-richardschulman.com
www.2transformation.com

THE LABYRINTH OF HEALING

The Emotional Shifting Process

_____

Richard G. Schulman, PhD

Table of Contents

ACKNOWLEDGEMENTS

The writing and editing of this manuscript has in many ways paralleled the healing journey through a labyrinth. I'd like to thank some of the people who guided and inspired me along the way.

First I'd like to thank my teachers from Psychology, Psychiatry, and Psychotherapy. Thank you James M. Anker, PhD, Jacqueline Becker, PhD, Donna Horn, PhD, Pauline Powers, MD, Lawrence Ricker, PhD, Brian Weiss, MD, and Eugene Zukowsky, PhD. Each of these people participated in my growth as a psychotherapist, and also cared deeply about the development of my soul. I send much gratitude and appreciation.

I would also like to thank the body therapists with whom I have worked with intensively over the years. Cat Taylor, LMT, Alice Quaid, PT, Liz Shands (now Blassingame), LMT, Jeffrey M. Hocker, LMT, Si, Angelique Bollietieri, AP, DOM, Adrienne Borden-Sundberg, AP, DOM, Kerry D'Ambrogio, AP, DOM, Sandy Couture LMT, and Richard VanBuskirk, DO, PhD, FAAO. I have learned something from each and every one of you. I appreciate your brilliance and support.

I would like to acknowledge teachers from other arenas of consciousness. Thanks to Yogi John McKenney for your steadfast support, expertise, and patience in teaching me Ashtanga Yoga. Thank you, Antonina Garcia, LCSW, EdD, for your brilliant instruction in Psychodrama. I send appreciation to Rev. Dr. James A. Meade, Msc.D., Hypnotherapist, who opened a new and bigger world for me. A posthumous thank you to Cmdr USN Arnold Lee Glass, Master Hypnotist, and so much more, for mentoring me about so many things.

Much appreciation goes out to the people who helped edit and correct this manuscript at various stages of its development: Allan Kurzrok, PhD, Linda Maree, Linda Ann Remley, CAP, and Laurie Rosen. Thanks to Carla Henshaw for being the midwife to the final push over the finish line in the birthing of this book. I send much appreciation to Sean Keenan for the beautiful artwork on the front and back covers and preparing the manuscript for publishing.

I have been inspired by many: Pete Townshend, Ram Dass, Chogyam Trungpa, Yogi David Swenson, Gene Roddenberry, Milton Erickson, MD, John Upledger, DO, Wilhelm Reich, MD, Stanislav Grof, MD, Harry Stack Sullivan, MD, Joseph Heller, Ursula LeGuin, Aldous Huxley, Issac Asimov, and many more.

I thank my children, Jonathan Schulman, MA, and Daniel Lee Schulman, for becoming the wonderful human beings they are, inspiring me that there is hope for a brighter future for humanity, and teaching me about love. I thank my parents, Bert and Evelyn Schulman, for sparking the quest for knowledge, providing models for creative expression, and their love and caring.

Special thanks goes to Brian A. Hill for teaching me the beautiful art of astrology, suggesting the title of this book, and for your unflagging support and love.

–RICHARD G. SCHULMAN, PHD

INTRODUCTION

LABYRINTH AND
EMOTIONAL HEALING

For millennia, the Labyrinth has been a symbol of wholeness, a place to reconnect with the depth of our soul and the core of our being. Walking the sacred geometry of the Labyrinth is akin to moving through the inner journey of life. The voyage is transformational and heroic.

By definition, a Labyrinth has one path that leads to the center and then out the same way. There are no dead ends, blind alleys, or turnarounds. Points that seem close to the goal actually reflect a longer distance for the seeker to travel. Once entered, the only requirement is to follow the path to the center without turning back and the only variable is the speed one travels.

Emotional healing is much like moving through a Labyrinth. The journey is simultaneously sought after and feared, and will contain both visible, as well as, invisible elements. A trial is undertaken and then an initiation into a new life comes about. Finally, a transformation, in which the seeker becomes hero takes place. Passage through the Labyrinth of Healing is a liberation holding meaning and creative life

You, the reader, stand at the entrance to the Labyrinth, a seeker holding all the possibilities and potential of the journey before you. The stories of my patients, body therapists, and I wait for you just inside the entryway. Travel the path lightly, taking only ideas, experiences, knowledge, relationships, and a mind ready for new learning.

If you are lost, you are not alone. Like Nomads in the desert, being lost is not the same as being defeated. You are encouraged to release old maladaptive patterns, ideas, and concepts that no longer serve you. You have an opportunity to cleanse your painful emotional memories and challenging behavioral interactions. I invite you to move forward through the portal and walk together with us on a path to the center of The Emotional Shifting Process, a paradigm for emotional healing, spiritual growth and transformation.

Richard G. Schulman, PhD
Sarasota, Florida
August 21, 2017

ENTRY: PSYCHOLOGY AND SOUL

*People do not come into therapy to
change their past, but their future.*
—Milton H Erickson

The term Psychology comes from the Greek words 'psyche' or soul and 'logos' or word, and literally means the expression of intelligence or the 'word' of the soul. The term psychotherapy comes from the words 'psyche' and 'therapeia' — "curing, healing, service done to the sick." During six years of graduate training in clinical psychology I studied concepts and theories of behavior, thought, belief, emotion, motivation, memory, perception, and learning, among others. I did not once hear the word "soul." As a clinical psychologist, my life's work has been about studying the word of the soul and providing service to the healing thereof.

The soul is a transcendent tapestry sewn from many threads. It is the totality that we bring with us to the earth upon our arrival. Soul includes the sum of our experiences and relationships traveling through time from the moment of our creation. Soul is as personal as a fingerprint or DNA matrix, and as all encompassing as the World Wide Web. Soul is individualistic and idiosyncratic, and yet connected to every being. Soul is interrelated with mind and body.

A mystery is carried within the soul that I engage in my role as psychologist with awe and respect. My reverence for the majesty of the soul has expanded as I have become aware of forces beyond the physical and material world that influence the feelings, behavior, thoughts, perception, and attitudes that accompany life events and can directly affect the outcome of these episodes.

I believe the the soul, rather than coming to earth as a tabula rasa or blank slate, brings with it intent and mission, an outline of what it would like to accomplish, as well as, the means to reach its purpose. Experiences like pain, illness, hunger, loneliness, and the emotional turmoil found in relationships provide motivation to access transformational energies. Heartfelt, emotional understanding of these events and circumstances allow our capacity for compassion (the empathy motivating a true desire to help relieve the suffering of others) to grow from a concept into an experiential reality.

Interpersonal interactions are the most common arena where soul challenges are met. Relationships provide the setting in which progress towards spiritual growth and healing is achieved. Our urgency to find a paradigm that will initiate and accelerate personal and interpersonal healing is powerful. To paraphrase psychologist Abraham Maslow, if you chose to be born in a Western culture like the United States or Europe, you will most likely not be doing your spiritual work meditating on a mountaintop. Maslow speculated that spiritual advancement in our society is accomplished by making our ordinary relationships into spiritual ones, and those who are successful in such efforts become Western civilization's version of Eastern mystics.

Spiritual transformation is not only for those who would scale the Himalayan peaks. If our goals regarding bonds and alliances with others are met, it becomes much easier for us to merge and balance our everyday existence with the peacefulness of spiritual life.

The spiritual techniques and understanding of the ancients are still valid, but must be integrated into our fast-paced, stressful, modern world. The call for meaning beyond the personal compels many to drink from the cup of the divine mystery as a way through these turbulent times. The need to repair the tears in the tapestry of our individual and collective soul is staggering.

The soul's nature is holistic, that is, in relationship with every part of the human being's essence and existence. This makes a poor fit for therapies that are increasingly specialized and tend to be exclusive rather than inclusive. Within the realm of emotional healing it is rare that conventional psychotherapies and transpersonal techniques are incorporated in an integrated, seamless manner.

Any therapist whose practice encourages patients to experience deep emotional or spiritual events may put those patients at risk for emotional injury, relationship difficulties, and family discord. The therapist's education must include a reasonably thorough study in psychology and the application of learned skills in psychotherapy. On the other hand, a conventional psychotherapist may try to exclude certain aspects of a patient's inner world and, in so doing, discourages the patient from receiving a potentially life transforming experience.

I advocate a holistic, soul-based psychotherapy. My approach incorporates a foundation of conventional psychological methods and theory, integrated with some of the less conventional concepts, techniques, and objectives. I have found, far from being mutually exclusive, the two perspectives can balance and complement each other most effectively. Established psychotherapeutic modalities can be used to internalize and incorporate the deepest discoveries that the less traditional procedures have uncovered. My own exploration in the service of this psychotherapeutic integration has brought me through experiences of individual, family and group psychotherapy, deep hypnotic realities, psychodrama, and eventually into the development of a technique whereby the body therapist and psychotherapist work simultaneously on the patient, called the Emotional Shifting Process. All of these methods and theories have created the Labyrinth of Healing.

The Emotional Shifting Process (E.S.P.) has been developed over many years with many different patients. A study was done to assess the efficacy of this technique (see Appendix A) and the data, as well as, comments made anonymously by patients point to overwhelmingly positive outcomes from this treatment approach. The technique has been used successfully to treat Post Traumatic Stress Disorder, anxiety disorders, depression, chronic pain, and a myriad of other psychiatric problems.

The patients and body therapists whose stories populate this manuscript are real people. All of the events described herein happened. Names and identifying information have been changed to protect the confidentiality of the individuals. Those who choose to go with me on this journey of self-knowledge are incredibly brave. The hardest thing we do as human beings is look in the mirror.

Rather than being interested in theories, however, patients are interested in results. I invite you to suspend your disbelief, slide into a beginner's mind, and walk with me on an expedition into the deep well of consciousness, the rarified air of spirit, and the power of the growth of human souls and their journey through The Labyrinth of Healing.

1. FOUNDATIONS OF A HOLISTIC PSYCHOTHERAPY

"Any sufficiently advanced technology is indistinguishable from magic."
–Arthur C. Clarke

Psychotherapy is a unique occurrence in the history of our species. The need for emotional well-being has either been largely ignored as man struggled for physical survival, or explained away as a reaction to normal suffering. For millennia, this was the purview of priests, rebbes, and shamans, who overlaid counseling with religious constructs or helped assign meaning to suffering. The task of emotional healing has moved into the arena of medicine and the science of psychology in the last century. The poorly defined art/science of psychotherapy covers a multiplicity of techniques, a number of radically different philosophies, and often yields unclear results.

As a young student of clinical psychology, I was devoted to learning the science of psychotherapy. The 1980s were a time when biological psychiatry was flowering with the advent of new anti-depressant medications, and academic psychology was ruled by cognitive-behaviorists. My training in psychotherapy, facilitated by several excellent teachers and mentors, began to unfold techniques of this healing modality that went beyond the ordinary academic and biological perspective. I was encouraged to listen to the music of a patient's life that lay underneath the words, to glean the patterns of behavior and interaction that would emerge if I allowed them to come to me. When I did, underlying themes and unconscious patterns of a patient's life became available for me to comment on and work with.

While in graduate school at the University of South Florida, watching a re-run of Star Trek (the original series), I saw Dr. McCoy's sickbay. There was a bed with many dials and readouts above it, providing immediate biological data on the status of the patient. Excitedly, I turned to one of my fellow students and said, "If I had one of those, I'd be the greatest therapist in the world. I'd know the inner truth of how each patient was reacting from their bodies." Looking back, perhaps this was the beginning of my quest to uncover, energize, and push the envelope of psychotherapeutic technique beyond anything I had been taught or had imagined.

The process of earning my doctorate in clinical psychology gave me a strong fundamental knowledge of psychology and the practice of psychotherapy. However, learning doesn't stop with a degree. I've spent many years reaching for new experiences, perspectives, and modalities while continuing to sharpen psychotherapy skills and techniques. One never knows which sliver of information, experience, or inspiration will make the difference in helping a patient. The magic is what is created for each individual patient and by it's very nature unique to that person.

One of my physician friends once told me that I had more arrows in my quiver than any psychologist he'd ever met. He said, "You try one thing, and if it doesn't work, you reach for another technique, another way of looking at things, until you find something that works." All the psychotherapeutic techniques that I have encountered have value when applied appropriately. Many different techniques and perspectives are employed in my work. Just as we wouldn't need major surgery for a hangnail, powerful interventions such as the Emotional Shifting Process are engaged when more conventional methods have failed to generate positive outcomes or clear the last vestiges of trauma from those who have participated in psychotherapy for years. The modality, timing, and dosage of any intervention is tailored to meet the unique needs and highest good of the patient.

The philosophical underpinnings of the work are simple if not easy to actualize. If the physical realities of gas, liquid, and solid exist in a continuum, then from my perspective, the psychological realities of thought, energy, and matter can be viewed as also existing in a continuum. I see thought as thin energy, and energy as thin matter. Behavior, emotion, and cognition interact with each other in patterns. Thoughts and beliefs form a filter through which a person sees the world. Repeating patterns of behavior, emotion, and interpersonal interaction create personality and life experience. Mind, body, and spirit occur simultaneously and are encoded in memory as such. The model is holistic in the deepest sense. So, if these forces happen as one, shouldn't we attempt to address them as such?

One of my patients told me long ago, "Dr. Schulman, you don't expect miracles, you demand them." For me, a miracle is what happens when a human being has a vision that is manifest in real time. A businesswoman with years of worsening flight phobia presented for an emergency session at the behest of her mother, a longtime patient. Previously, she'd needed copious amounts of alcohol mixed with Valium in order to be able to fly. She expressed dismay as she showed me a roster of flights involving upcoming travel. After one session, she has been able to travel by air comfortably. She returned for a session this year to happily report no recurrence of symptoms. She described what happened as a miracle. I am grateful that her subconscious mind revealed the origin of her difficulties and allowed me to access them to facilitate feeling.

The power to heal implies a power to hurt. A scalpel in the hands of a skilled surgeon can save one's life, but in the hands of a mugger can end life. Psychotherapy is a powerful tool for emotional healing. Due to the fact that it is powerful and patients are vulnerable, the practice of psychotherapy is regulated by state licensing boards. Licensure and training define the scope of practice for anyone in the healing arts. Licensure requires the licensee attend an accredited training program with defined academic coursework and supervised clinical practice. This will be true no matter if one's license is that of a psychologist, psychiatrist, social worker, mental health counselor, or marriage and family therapist. Completing the licensure process gives a level of confidence for patients that the practitioner has basic knowledge of the science of psychology and psychotherapy.

If emotional wounds are created in relationship, they are more effectively healed in an interactive process. This is what gives psychotherapy its healing power. Psychotherapy is a relationship defined expressly for that purpose. My psychotherapy teacher, Dr. James Anker, told me there were only two issues in psychotherapy. Dr. Anker's first issue was, "How do you get in?" His second issue was, "What do you do when you are there?" These are simple questions, without easy answers.

Psychotherapy, practiced well, is an elegant, beautiful technique. From my perspective, the process of psychotherapy incorporates elements of science, dance, music, martial arts, and theatre. Effective psychotherapy involves integrating knowledge from the science of psychology with the realities of emotional connection between individuals. Artistic endeavors have always had the potential of activating the observer's inner world, and may be used with great power and effectiveness in psychotherapy.

The process of psychotherapy is as vast as the patient's needs for connection and understanding. Knowing the psychological foundations of cognitive and emotional development, having a background in psychological testing, diagnostic categorization, family dynamics, learning, memory, perception, and motivation are necessary, but not sufficient. One has to know the rules before one can bend or break them. Since communication is often based more on body language and tone of voice than on the words themselves, the well-trained psychotherapist is indispensable for emotional healing processes.

It has been my experience that psychotherapy should be taught in an apprenticeship model, including face-to-face supervision of the therapist by experienced teachers. The reason this is so important is that mistakes made by a psychotherapist often occur unconsciously. It takes an outside observer to identify mistakes and provide correction. This model employs the lineage handed down from trainer to trainee to patient and includes all of the experiences, observations, and learning built on the knowledge going back to the first teacher.

The father of modern psychotherapy is Sigmund Freud. My work is deeply indebted to Dr. Freud for providing the concepts of the subconscious mind, psychological repression, defense mechanisms, dream interpretation, and the role of early experience. Freud opened the discussion of the need for healthy sexuality. He identified the idea of transference, or the placing of feelings for a significant person in a patient's life onto the psychotherapist, as well as, counter transference, the therapist's emotional entanglement with the patient. As much as Freud provided, I was left wanting more.

Harry Stack Sullivan is one of my psychotherapy

heroes. Sullivan identified the idea of parataxic distortion as the process whereby perceptions of the patient are skewed by their projection onto the therapist. This is different from Freud's view of transference in that Freud felt that transference developed slowly over time, while for Sullivan, parataxic distortion happened immediately, a reflection of how the patient interacts with other important people in his or her life. Sullivan advocated addressing these interactions in the moment, during the session. For Sullivan, the psychotherapy session became about the here and now, rather than the there and then. Sullivan looked for repeating patterns of interaction and behavior. He believed those difficulties in interpersonal relationships were deeply human experiences, exclusive of diagnostic constriction.

I remember walking back from lunch with Dr. Anker and passing an obviously impaired man on the street. When we got back to his office, Dr. Anker questioned me. "Mr. Schooolman," he intoned with some theatricality, "What was the diagnosis of the man we saw in the street?" "Schizophrenia, probably, catatonic type," I replied. "Good," he answered. "Now, I'll ask you a more important question," he continued. "How is that man any different from you?" I deliberated for a moment, and then said, "Quantity of symptoms." Dr. Anker nodded affirmatively. "If you ever think you are different from that man, or any patient, it's time to give up practice. We are all more human than anything else."

Sullivan also described the therapist role as one of participant/observer. As psychotherapist, I participate in the therapeutic relationship and also observe it. In the Emotional Shifting Process, both the body therapist and the psychotherapist participate jointly with the patient, while I, as the psychotherapist, observe and facilitate the therapeutic interactions. The process is by its nature highly charged emotionally, and is rich with opportunity for emotional processing.

Carl Jung brought the notion of spirituality to psychotherapy. Jung's cross cultural studies of archetypes, or universal symbols reflecting emotional development and expression, provided a brilliant foundation for the spiritual perspective vital to deep psychological exploration. Jung also gave us the concept of anima and animus (male and female energies we all contain inside of us) and the idea of the collective unconscious. Jung gave us the spirit, but did not include the body.

Wilhelm Reich was the great genius from Freud's roundtable who included the body, the politics, and the role of orgasm and energy as issues to be considered in the quest for emotional healing. Reichian thought is an underpinning for many body-oriented techniques, such as Somato-Emotional Release and Rolfing. Reich described armoring in the body. This body armor is encountered during the Emotional Shifting Process on a regular basis. His theories are a foundation for my own journey into mind-body therapies.

The Family Systems model looks at the family as the primary place for healing and growth. The family develops a homeostatic process that delineates and regulates interactive behavior in the system. The process defines roles and emotional expression that maintain emotional functioning in the family, which are at times maladaptive. Understanding family dynamics and creating interventions based on those interactive processes can be powerful catalysts for healing in the therapeutic endeavor.

Stanislav Grof, a Czech psychiatrist, was one of the early researchers into LSD. Grof advocated the processing of birth trauma and deep psycho-spiritual events impacting emotional functioning. He developed the technique of Holotropic Breathwork to investigate this facet of the emotional landscape. Holotropic Breathwork is an intense process involving yogic breathing; evocative high intensity music, bodywork, and art work to access deep emotional material. Dr. Grof's ideas greatly expanded the field of psychological inquiry, offering the additional metaphors of birth, and the intrauterine world into the psychotherapeutic exploration.

If we add up the ideas and techniques of these giants and include the conventional foundations of psychological functioning, such as learning, memory, perception, and motivation, and throw in psychotherapeutic experience and skill, the mountain one needs to climb to become a well prepared psychotherapist looms large. Add family and behavioral therapies, all the lessons of hypnosis (more on this later), neurolinguistic programming, eye movement, tapping therapies, music, poetry, literature, theatre, film, television, other arts, and one begins to get an idea of how the therapist must be prepared for just about anything. The psychotherapist must be ready to provide a model of the universe that is suited to the patient's particular worldview, personal symbolism, and needs.

While my perspective on psychotherapy, including the Emotional Shifting Process, has at its core a holistic philosophy, there are specific skills, knowledge, and experience for the psychotherapist and the body therapist vital to facilitate positive outcomes for the patient. The database the therapist brings into the healing theatre will vastly affect the results. Good intentions are not enough.

In a true mind-body approach, the demands of psychotherapy are too specialized and intensive to be practiced while simultaneously taking care of the body. Monitoring the body while the patient is experiencing emotional events is too much to do while one is maintaining a dialog. The different skill sets and experience needed to participate in the process successfully make a team approach sensible and practical. Imagine going into surgery and having the surgeon act as the anesthesiologist, nurse, etc. . .

Experience on an inpatient psychiatric setting is invaluable for a holistic psychotherapist. The inpatient psychiatric setting takes the practitioner to the edges of human emotional experience. If you don't know where the edges are, it is difficult to know the middle. This helps guard against overreacting to patient presentation of complaints. In such an intense venue, the extremes of behavior, emotion, and thought disturbance can be studied directly. The visceral nature of the experience creates a powerful environment for learning about the patient as a human being, rather than diagnostic entities. Conventional psychological testing may also offer important information to be integrated into the treatment process. This includes personality, intelligence, and neuropsychological testing materials.

An understanding of brain to behavior relationship has the potential to be a factor in understanding and treating psychological problems. All evidence as to cause and consequence of emotional difficulties must be considered through the lens of brain function, physical health, and medications if applicable. In addition, people feel their emotions all over the body. Gut feelings, tightening of the throat, and pain that physical examination cannot explain are commonly reported. The therapist's awareness that emotion is processed all over the body, rather than just in the brain, is vital for successful therapeutic outcomes.

Experience working with people of all ages and problems, in as many varied settings as possible, is also quite helpful. Developmental issues change throughout our lives. An anxiety ridden 25 year old dealing with a new child will have a different experience of life than a depressed 70 year old coping with illness or the death of a spouse.

Psychotherapeutic skill, knowledge, and experience are likely the most important components of the process. In addition, due to the fact that every patient has his or her own idiosyncratic model of the universe, understanding different ways to conceptualize a case (whether it be from a Freudian, Jungian, Sullvanian, Reichian, Behavioral, Cognitive, Family Systems perspective), provides the flexibility of thought that facilitates a psychotherapists ability to flow with the patient, while at the same time providing guidance and support to the journey.

Familiarity with, and understanding of trance phenomena, is vital to my model, even if one does not employ hypnosis. Techniques such as, creative visualization, regression phenomena, time distortion and progression use information about how a patient accesses his or her inner world and imagination. Brain scan studies have shown that visualization of an object or event will show similar, if not exactly identical, brain activity as experiencing the same object or event in reality. Some of this information can be found in Neurolinguistic Programming techniques.

Knowledge of eye movement techniques, such as EMDR (Eye Movement Desensitization and Reprocessing), and tapping therapies such as EFT (Emotional Freedom Technique) are useful, as well. Eye movement and tapping facilitate corrective emotional learning experiences by allowing patients to access strong emotional material, while disrupting maladaptive patterns of brain activity and emotional processing.

The use of music, art, literature, poetry, history, and cinema will also facilitate the psychotherapist's ability to connect with the patient at a deep level. Individuals will often attach an emotional event to a song, i.e. after a breakup, a couple will find it very painful to hear 'our song' that they danced to at their wedding party.

The psychotherapist, while not responsible for the body part of the process, must understand the idea that there is no real separation among the mind, body, and spirit. Knowledge of subtle energy, or energy medicine, as described by Richard Gerber, MD, will ease communication between the body therapist and psychotherapist, and support the smooth functioning of the therapeutic process.

Eastern medical approaches, such as acupuncture, provide information and delineation of mind-body relationships. As a psychotherapist, I don't know prior to session what approach will give me the key to healing, but I want to be prepared for the patient's own symbolism reflecting his or her inner world.

For the body therapist who wishes to participate in the Emotional Shifting Process, basic fundamental understanding of the body is essential. Programs involved in training massage therapists, physical therapists, acupuncture physicians, and chiropractors, provide strong fundamental information and training. Knowledge of anatomy and physiology are prerequisites to working at the more subtle levels. The understanding of energy medicine is key for the body therapist who wants to work with the Emotional Shifting Process, as well. Dealing with subtle and emotional energies requires extreme sensitivity to minute changes in body functioning.

Knowledge and experience with soft tissue techniques, such as Craniosacral Therapy and Myofascial Release, will strongly support the body therapy portion of the Emotional Shifting Process. Craniosacral Therapy uses gentle touch of the cranial bones as 'handles' to manipulate the soft tissue to release energetic blockages that improve the flow of energy throughout the Central Nervous System. Myofascial Release uses several different protocols, some with strong pressure, others with gentle prolonged touch, all of which attempt to facilitate release of energy stored in the connective tissue by elongating or stretching the fascia.

There must be a shared philosophy of how the process works and a respect for what each professional brings to the therapy session. Still, because this is an emotion based therapy, the psychotherapist, with the input from the body therapist, must make the final decisions regarding timing and level of interventions.

Stepping back to look at the enormous amount of material that one needs to incorporate in order to practice mind-body therapy is a daunting experience. However, it is not so different from the process a surgeon, fighter pilot, master musician, or professional athlete has to go through in order to practice, fly, or play at a high level. The outcome is worth the effort.

For over three decades, I have had the privilege of watching a parade of humanity pass in front of me during my tens of thousands of hours of psychotherapy practice. I remain in awe of the mystery. My work stands on the shoulders of giants such as Sigmund Freud, Carl Jung, Harry Stack Sullivan, Wilhelm Reich, Stanislav Grof, Brian Weiss, and Milton Erickson, to name a few. We are on a journey together into The Labyrinth, a world of emotional healing and the psychotherapeutic perspectives, methods, and techniques that when used harmoniously, and wisely, have created positive outcomes, becoming miracles of healing and growth for my patients.

2. PROCESS
AND TECHNIQUE:
TOUCH AND TALK

"Touch has a memory."
–John Keats

The Emotional Shifting Process is a therapeutic modality involving the simultaneous participation of both psychotherapist and body therapist in the session to help a patient release and process deep emotional issues. The psychotherapist is responsible for the dialogue and processing of emotional material, while the body therapist monitors bodily reactions to the material and facilitates the release of emotion trapped within the body. In this chapter I describe the philosophy of the Emotional Shifting Process, how a session might look, and take you through two case histories to demonstrate the power and potential of this modality for emotional healing.

Ron: The Navy SEAL with Back Pain

Ron, one of the first patients who participated in the Emotional Shifting Process, was in his late forties at the time. He had been a Navy SEAL, serving three tours of duty in Vietnam. For years after returning from the war, he appeared to be relatively well adjusted and productive. Then, one day at work, he slipped and fell in a puddle of water, a seemingly minor accident. From that point on, however, he suffered chronic pain, dizziness, anxiety, and depression. The physicians he consulted during the next two years were unable to diagnose the cause of Ron's symptoms. Meanwhile, his life was falling apart.

When Ron first came to my office, I noticed he would likely be an excellent hypnotic subject. He could roll his eyes back into his head so that mostly white was showing, a behavior often correlated with good hypnotic susceptibility. As it turned out, he could attain a deep trance state with remarkable ease. When hypnotized, he would relax deeply and feel better, but his symptoms would return to their pre-trance levels as soon as the session ended. Because he was unable to sustain the relief he felt during the hypnotherapy sessions, Ron agreed to try the Emotional Shifting Process.

In a small massage room, with a soft light creating a relaxed atmosphere, Ron, physical therapist, Grace Walters, and myself, as a three-person team began to explore Ron's pain. Ron lay on his back on the table, while Grace was seated behind him, her hand gently resting on his shoulder. Although there was a chair for me, I chose to stand, yellow pad in hand, and the dialogue began. I asked Ron to begin with his most recent injury.

He spoke about the slip and fall in which he was injured. That led into a discussion of his dissatisfaction with his job situation. His negativity was compounded by the work difficulties arising from the physical impairment due to his pain. While it seemed likely from my initial conversations with Ron that the origin of his problems could be traced to his wartime experience in Vietnam, he was reluctant to discuss it. "That was a long time ago," he protested, adding that for over a decade after the war he had not encountered any serious physical or emotional problems.

I knew from my year of training as an intern at the VA hospital in Palo Alto, California, the majority of Post Traumatic Stress Disorder patients were reluctant to discuss their trauma. As one might expect, this very intelligent, articulate, and rational patient was expert in citing reasons for avoiding the topic. I suggested to Ron his injury on the job could have triggered problems that had merely been dormant. Despite the misgivings he voiced regarding speaking about the war, he was willing to explore the notion that the severity of his symptoms could not be explained by a simple slip and fall. He agreed to dig deeper into his own psyche.

After the first three sessions were completed, we learned Ron had suffered a variety of profoundly troubling events during the war. Two in particular seemed to have had the greatest impact: his guilt from surviving a helicopter crash that had taken the lives of many of his buddies, and the torment he was subjected to as a veteran after he returned to the United States. For those readers too young to understand what happened during the Vietnam War, returning soldiers were often treated abominably. War protesters sometimes spat at the troops and called them "baby killers' just as they were disembarking from their flights back to the United States.

During one Emotional Shifting Process session, Grace and I uncovered the power of his survivor's guilt. Ron was squirming around on the table, attempting to find a comfortable position for himself, when Grace signaled to me that he spontaneously assumed a significant body position. "The pain is horrific as always." he said. "Why do you even bother to ask?"

I suggested Ron focus on the posture his body was in and allow the pain to tell him where it was coming from. He had unconsciously moved his body into a position in which he was sitting on the table, knees pulled up close to his body, cradling his arms around them. Almost immediately, he realized he had duplicated the very same position troops were required to maintain on transport helicopters in Vietnam. He spontaneously recalled the specific incident that had been so traumatic. Ron was onboard one of two helicopters loaded with wounded American soldiers. He proudly explained how the SEALs never leave a wounded comrade behind, no matter the situation. While he spoke, his body began to vibrate as if he were actually in the helicopter.

Responding to the cue, Grace slid in behind him on the table, supporting his back, and began gently rocking his body back and forth, attempting to reproduce, as closely as possible under the circumstances, the feeling of being in the chopper. Ron's commander ordered him to get out of the helicopter and board the other one. He complied immediately and ran to the other helicopter. An instant later, he watched in horror as the helicopter he had just left was torn apart by an enemy rocket, killing everyone aboard.

As Grace held him, Ron's body convulsed, reflecting the emotional shock he felt in watching the horrifying wartime scene. This, apparently, was the source of the torrent of pain activated by his fall at work. He wept as the tight body shield he had created to keep his emotions in check melted away. He talked about his dead friends, how they had put their lives on the line for him in the jungle, and how he should have died with them. Then he angrily recalled how anti-war protesters spat at him when he returned home from the war. He was so enraged that he threw his bronze star into the Potomac River.

As he released these memories, Ron's body softened noticeably. He appeared to open like a blooming flower. His shoulders grew wider before our eyes; the lines of worry and tension so evident on his face at the start of the session relaxed. In a quiet voice, Ron told us he wasn't in as much pain as before.

While this session hadn't provided a lightning cure, Ron had discovered a new path, one in which his ultimate healing was at least a possibility. His physical pain had been an indication the severe mental traumas he had experienced had somehow lodged in his body. The release and relief he experienced gave him hope and inspiration he could improve and supported him in his recovery. His emotional well being improved almost immediately. He was subsequently able to participate with determination and positivity in an exercise program designed to increase strength and flexibility. He returned to work and began to enjoy life again. His pain, once devastating, became manageable.

In our present day, we live in a touch-starved, touch-phobic society. Touch creates a dramatic emotional connection with another person, whether it is good, positive touch or violent, negative touch. Trauma often has its origin in the body. One of the main advantages of the Emotional Shifting Process is how the team approach integrates touch in the service of emotional healing.

The body has been included in psychotherapeutic interventions, most notably the techniques espoused by Wilhelm Reich, MD, and his student Alexander Lowen, MD, father of Bioenergetics. Osteopathic medicine has long recognized the idea of somato-emotional release, which describes an emotional reaction to manipulation that releases emotional energies from the body. Traditional Chinese medicine has, at its core, a philosophy and modality that identifies the pathways of energy in the body known as meridians, and the physical consequences when the flow of life energy, also referred to as Chi, is blocked. I have often heard body therapists comment, "Bones heal and tissue remembers."

Therapists who identify themselves as body psychotherapists, are typically psychotherapists who have some level of insight and experience with the body, or body therapists who have some level of training in dialogue. I was appalled to hear a famous physician describe the therapeutic dialog in his technique as 'only a conversation.'

Body therapists are rarely well trained in psychotherapy techniques, while psychotherapists are often bereft of body knowledge. In practical application, tracking all of the many aspects that come into play when a patient is in the throes of emotional processing is extremely difficult. Again, it's as if one were doing surgery and had to be the surgeon, anesthesiologist, and nurse all at once. The Emotional Shifting Process combines the efforts of the psychotherapist and body therapist working in tandem to give the patient a more comprehensive vehicle for emotional growth and healing.

The Emotional Shifting Process uses the monitoring of body reactions as a very sensitive meter to determine how the patient is responding to the therapeutic dialogue. The body therapist becomes, in essence, the ultimate emotional biofeedback instrument. Since body position sometimes dictates the release, the body therapist has to be adept at gentle manipulation and sensitive as to the best position for the release. Body based interventions such as eye movement (EMDR) and tapping (EFT), techniques gleaned from Neurolinguistic Programming and kinesiology, may also be incorporated into the technique.

My long time friend and co-therapist, Carol Martin, described the experience: "When I put my hand on the patient, I'm plugged into the energy. Keeping my hand on someone allows me to feel the energy nuances of the body. When you actually have your hand on someone for an hour it tells you a lot about the person. The shifts become more apparent in the energy patterns. I can compare the patient's tone of voice to the body reaction. If the tone feels wrong, I'm not the one who is reacting, it's the energy coming off their body that shows me the discrepancy."

Carol's training in massage therapy, craniosacral therapy, and other energetic techniques provided her a way of interpreting and working with the body at a very sensitive level. It is my observation that she is dealing with micro expressions of the body that a person without her training and experience would almost certainly miss.

In the event of a trauma, the impact on mind, body, heart, and spirit are all encoded in memory simultaneously. The body's reaction to the circumstance of trauma may result in it being stuck in an unhealthy shape. An unhealthy shape can be seen as emotionally determined and 'remembered' by the body. Many sufferers of chronic pain will report going to a chiropractor or massage therapist and receive temporary relief, but within 24 to 48 hours, the pain returns. As in Ron's situation, the body remembers the trauma at a deeper level, and subsequently returns to the stance of holding the emotional pain causing irritation from misalignment.

When a physical injury is caused by a traumatic event, the emotions generated by the experience may be imprinted on that part of the body or referred to another location in the body. The idea that stored emotional energy is blocking normal energetic flow describes what is often seen clinically when working with patients. This can occur with or without a specific physical injury. Recounting the event or events during a psychotherapeutic dialogue while having the body engaged therapeutically can release the energy held by the body and result in an improvement in health (as seen in pain reduction) and an increase in emotional well being.

Part of what transforms the traumatic imprint is while the release is occuring, the patient is experiencing the gentle, supportive touch of the body therapist. Emotional expression is encouraged and supported by the psychotherapist. The psychotherapist then assists integration of emotional material in the context of a positive emotional and physical environment.

The interaction between psychotherapist and body therapist is key in getting beyond the patient's armor and into the emotional material that lies below. The body therapist, in essence, provides very useful raw data from a physical, as well as, an energetic perspective. The reactions of the body to emotional material give powerful information, often identifying specific ages in the patient's history, and relationships to explore. The psychotherapist must synthesize and translate all of this information for patient consumption.

Once significant information from the patient has been revealed, the psychotherapist must maintain what is called 'the emotional field' for the session. Ideally, the emotional field is one of permission and protection, a safe space in which the patient feels free to express, or not express, his or her inner world without fear of humiliation or retribution.

The reaction of a therapist at the moment a patient opens an inner emotional world can heal or harm. Most people, especially patients with psychiatric problems, have been programmed since childhood to believe their feelings are, at best, inconvenient, or at worst, terrifying and destructive. The moment of emotional opening is precisely the point where psychotherapeutic experience, skill, and technique are of utmost importance to achieve a positive outcome.

While therapists cannot reasonably be expected to leave all their emotional baggage at the door in any conventional sense, they must remain keenly aware of their own emotions and guard against negatively influencing the process. Personally, if I feel my own emotions are getting in the way of the session, I momentarily step back, recognize the feelings, breathe deeply, and allow myself to release them. The awareness of and coping with my own emotional reactions to patient material is vital, but not always an easy process to engage. Learning how to deal with feelings towards patients is a hallmark of good psychotherapy training and critical for success.

Once a psychotherapist and body therapist have decided to work as a team, they must strive to integrate their efforts. The attitude they cultivate and project must be one of genuine mutual respect. In addition, both therapists must share a high degree of philosophical agreement regarding the nature of the work at hand.

The Emotional Shifting Process Session

Prior to the initiation of the Emotional Shifting Process, I often have what seems like small talk with the patient for a few moments. Although on the surface this conversation appears ordinary, it is not. This initial chatter not only relaxes the patient, but also provides me with a means to indirectly assess where the patient is emotionally and at times what he or she is ready to work on. An Emotional Shifting Process session then typically begins with the patient lying in a prone position on a massage table. The body therapist may sit or stand at the head of the table, gently holding the patient's head, touching his or her shoulder, or otherwise physically and energetically connecting with the patient.

Once the patient is comfortable, I begin a therapeutic dialogue, usually by inquiring what issues the patient wishes to explore. At the same time, the body therapist focuses on bodily processes, such as tension/relaxation, fluid movement, and energetic activity revealing inner emotional information.

The body therapist also monitors the Information Detector (I.D.). I'll have more to say about the I.D. later. For now, please understand that the I.D. is an interpretation by the body therapist of body signals as to what information is emotionally significant to the patient. It is not a lie detector or truth detector, only a detector of what is significant at that moment. The body therapist may signal to me the patient is ready, or may tell me her impressions of what the body is relaying. I then continue the therapeutic dialogue.

Sometimes, as the patient begins the session, I will

ask him or her to scan places in the body that may hold specific emotions in the form of a sense of awareness, or physical sensation, such as, pain or discomfort. Once the patient identifies a location, he or she is asked to describe it in detail, as if it were an object with material form. At that point, the focus the patient has on the inner world initiates the sequence of events that ultimately allows the release of the emotional energy. If a particular era in the life of that individual is targeted as ripe for examination, then the patient is asked to imagine what his or her life was like at that time. He or she can be encouraged to speak about the details of everyday life, e.g. the town in which the patient lived, the school attended, the house, or the rooms of the home, as examples of what may activate memory. As the patient describes the places, people, and events that made up life during this time period, I look for emotional reactivity. The patient may show subtle changes in breathing, move his or her body position, clench a fist, or get misty eyed. He or she may exhibit an even more overt emotional reaction, such as crying or pounding on the therapeutic table. The creative part of the therapeutic session really takes off when this emotional wellspring is tapped and the patient begins to connect feelings with thoughts and behavioral patterns.

Often, this is a time when the body therapist can facilitate the release of emotion that has been lodged in the patient's body. A healing touch at a critical moment can be enormously therapeutic in that effort. The energy of emotion in the body can even crystallize into islands of emotional energy being held prisoner in the body, encapsulated in the way a physical cyst forms a pocket of infection. The body frequently begins to divest itself of this material as we connect with deeper and deeper pools of emotion. As this emotion finds an avenue to vent itself, the energy cyst can be discharged. There have been occasions when I have been called upon to assist the body therapist, who directed me to facilitate the release of an energy cyst. The feeling of movement when the energy is released is remarkable for both patient and therapist. It's as though a swarm of bees were buzzing through my hands.

Patricia's Mysterious Cough

Patricia was a fifty-eight-year-old widow whose husband had died of stomach cancer after four miserable years of pain. Within a month of his death she developed a cough severe enough for her to seek medical help. The cough persisted over a period of months. Patricia went from doctor to doctor looking for relief. No cause was found and no satisfactory treatment was offered. Though the cough was clearly a physical problem, Patricia was convinced her symptoms had an emotional origin. After hearing her story, I suggested that the Emotional Shifting Process might prove helpful. Massage therapist, Carol Martin worked with me on this case.

During her first session, Patricia writhed on the table like a snake. In fact, her movements were extreme. She seemed awash in a vast reservoir of emotion. She coughed incessantly, yet was unable to tell us why she was coughing. She did say she felt the coughing was somehow connected to the release of emotion, that it somehow provided her with a sense of relief. During her second session, Patricia reported a change in her symptoms. Oddly, she reported that her cough would stop whenever she was on the phone, but would resume immediately once she hung up.

I asked Patricia to be as still as possible on the therapy table so that I could try to determine how her emotions were linked to her physical symptoms, to form an inner map of the cough. We accomplished this by asking a series of yes/no questions and the body therapist used the I.D. to ascertain the body's reactions to the questions. The body always tells the deeper truth of the patient. As we worked through a series of very specific questions (such as 'Did the point of origin of the cough occur before age 10?'), we found that Patricia's cough could be traced to age 13. Suddenly, a broad smile etched itself across her face and she began to giggle.

"What's so funny?" I asked.

"I didn't tell you before, because it didn't seem important," she replied, "but I had an emergency tonsillectomy at 13."

"An emergency tonsillectomy?" I asked curiously.

Thinking about it, Patricia allowed that she might be confusing her tonsillectomy with an appendectomy, a true emergency, she underwent at age seven. Acknowledging this as a possibility, I told her that we would try to verify the dates on which each of the surgeries took place. In response to a different set of questions, her body responses once again took us to age 13.

I encouraged Patricia to recall her tonsillectomy. She calmly recounted going to the hospital, getting ready for bed the night prior to the procedure, entering into the operating room, and going through the surgery. Then, without warning, Patricia burst into tears and sat up on the table.

She recalled being in her hospital bed after the surgery and feeling the urge to urinate. She rang the nurse's call button, but no one answered. She tried calling out, but her throat was too sore to make much of a sound. Finally, when the need to relieve herself grew unbearable, she got up to go to the bathroom. After a few wobbly steps, she collapsed. Lying on the floor of the hospital room, she felt dizzy, and began to vomit blood. Fortunately, a hospital orderly happened past her room, saw her on the floor, and quickly summoned a nurse. Patricia was immediately transported to the emergency room, where an attending physician inserted a tube down her throat, and pumped the blood that she had swallowed from her stomach.

As she relived this experience, Patricia began to cough violently. The memory that had been stuck within her body had been activated. She described the terror she had experienced and how she feared she would die. Then she remembered the guilt she felt at having disobeyed her doctor by getting out of bed without assistance. Her entire body shook as the energy attached to these feelings dissipated. When she calmed herself, Patricia sat on the edge of the therapeutic table, quietly speaking of her experience. She said, "Doc, I'm going to take a long shot. I spent four years taking my cancer-stricken husband to emergency rooms and having doctors who wouldn't listen to us. I think those experiences reminded me of that night, after my tonsillectomy, when no one could hear me."

This breakthrough heralded a time of tremendous growth and healing for Patricia. Her cough subsided completely for a while, and then returned, infrequently and in a mild form, usually as a sign that she was upset about something in her life. She even welcomed the cough, seeing it as a helpful messenger alerting her to some inner turmoil.

Over the next few months, she learned to express emotions more effectively. The symptom seemed to vanish completely, at least for the period of time I was treating her. Had it not been for the body therapist's sensitivity to the minute changes in the body in response to emotional challenges, we would not have detected the origin of Patricia's trauma. Neither time alone, nor traditional medicine, was likely to have brought the same level of symptom relief achieved through the Emotional Shifting Process.

Over the years I have worked with osteopathic physicians, acupuncture physicians, physical therapists, occupational therapists, and massage therapists as co-therapists in the session. As a psychotherapist interested in results, the information and modalities provided by the body therapist greatly increases my ability to function effectively as a facilitator of emotional healing. The additional data I have at my disposal empowers the work in qualitative ways. The sensation for me as psychotherapist is as if I had been watching black and white television and was then introduced to 3D Imax Technicolor.

In my practice, the Emotional Shifting Process is an extraordinarily powerful technique in opening opportunities for growth and healing. I regard my participation in the process as both a privilege and a responsibility. I imagine I have the soul of the patient in my hands and am determined to never drop it.

3. PATTERNS
AND MEANING

"From the moment of my birth
To the instant of my death,
There are patterns I must follow
Just as I must breathe each breath."
–Paul Simon

Human beings are by necessity creatures of pattern. Learning the rhythms and patterns of life tell us when to plant and harvest our crops, when to feed our livestock, and when to pray to the heavens. Learning patterns means we need not reinvent the wheel on a regular basis. Our bodies also run a number of different patterns, which include heart beat, blood pressure, craniosacral pulse, body temperature, and circadian rhythms to name a few.

The psyche is set up to create patterns even when none exist. In the 1930s psychologist Wolfgang Metzger studied the effect of staring into a featureless field of vision. Under these conditions, subjects began to hallucinate and their EEG readings changed significantly. This phenomenon, known as the Ganzfeld effect (German for 'complete field'), occurs due to the brain amplifying neural white noise in order to look for missing visual signals; in other words, looking for a pattern. The students of Pythagoras meditated in very deep caves where no light could reach to receive visions. Explorers in whiteout conditions have reported hallucinations, as did miners trapped without light by mining accidents.

Psychotherapy has long made use of patterns. A complete field of study and therapy revolves around family systems. The family system describes a homeostasis; that is, regulatory emotional rules that keep certain emotional patterns in place. It's as if each family member has a fixed role and definite lines in a play. Harry Stack Sullivan coined the phrase parataxic distortion to describe how an individual will unconsciously distort relationships to conform to earlier patterns learned in childhood.

Many of us have had the experience of looking back at our relationships only to later realize that we have connected with basically the same person in a different costume. As the troubadour once intoned, "My wives three, the only thing they had in common... was me." There are many patterns that people run in their lives, some conscious, most unconscious.

I worked with a family in which the presenting problem was violent arguments between the older daughter and her mother. In session, the daughter loudly ripped into her mother. When I intervened and blocked her from doing so, her younger sister took up where she left off, being rude and obnoxious to the mother. When I got the daughters to be quiet, I asked, "what would we be talking about if we weren't talking about this?" The younger girl replied simply, "That Dad is a f*cking drunk."

Upon a further review, we found that the mother was raised in an alcoholic family and her father was a particularly abusive drunk. She had unconsciously recreated the pattern of her family of origin in her current circumstances.

As a psychotherapist trained in the tradition of Harry Stack Sullivan's Interpersonal Psychotherapy, one of my goals is to pick up patterns that are unfolding in the room. Holly was a 58 year old female patient who had severe substance abuse problems, likely covering lifelong difficulties with anxiety and depression. As we dove into the therapy, I felt blocked off, as if I couldn't access the information I needed to help her. Holly had been describing communication difficulties in her family of origin. I realized those fragmented interactions were happening right in front of me. I said, "I feel like we are in that communication pattern right at this moment." She laughed sadly, and said, "Yep, it feels just like my family." That intervention loosened her up enough to begin to deal with the mother who would never listen to her.

It's Not Safe To Express Yourself

Tim, a 47 year old physician, avoided confrontation at all costs, which created problems in his practice. He had great difficulty in dealing with patients who did not follow his treatment regimen, and was frustrated and depressed with his situation. He was repeating a pattern from his family of origin where he was not allowed to express feelings, needs, or wants. When he realized he was acting out a childhood program of "It's not safe to express myself," he was able to let go of the repressed energies. He was also able to learn simple but powerful means of appropriate confrontation.

Robert and Lois Live in Each Others Wound

Robert and Lois were a couple who presented with serious communication difficulties brought about by what I call, "living in each other's wound." Robert grew up in a family with a lot of angry yelling and intimidation. Lois' family of origin dealt with problems with stone silence. Robert's pattern was to meet stress quietly, as he hated the loud arguing. Lois coped with stressful situations in the opposite manner, by being loud and argumentative. Being silent brought up tremendous anxiety for her. Disrupting the pattern as it emerged in session was extremely helpful in getting them to interact in a more appropriate, mature manner.

Dianne Keeps Everything Inside

For Dianne, a 53 year old, divorced woman, the pattern was to keep everything inside. She had been molested as a young girl by her uncle and warned that if she shared her secret, the family would break up. She had repressed the material to such an extent that she had no memory of it until a few years before our session. It weighed on her heavily in terms of depression and failed relationships. She had never talked about it with previous therapists. Having Carol and myself in the room together, made her feel as though she had the opportunity to express herself to her own parents. She was able to connect with her feelings and have permission to express them to her therapeutic "mother and father;" a different and healing way of doing things for her.

Meaning and Psychotherapy

Aldous Huxley once said, "Experience is not what happens to you, it's how you interpret what happens to you." How do we reach that holy grail of psychotherapy, the inner truth of a human being? In simpler terms, how does the therapist accurately access the reality of the patient's inner world? In the mid 1960s, a psychology professor at UCLA, Albert Mehrabian, studied communication. He found that much of communication is expressed by body language and tone of voice, while the words chosen had much less of an impact than had been previously thought, unless the person is expressing feelings.

Everyone has had the experience of saying the word "yes" while shaking our heads "no", or saying the word "no" while nodding our heads "yes". In psychotherapeutic technique these movements are known as meta-communication and could refer to any kind of body language.

Hypnotists have long used the phenomenon called levitation, in which a patient in trance would imagine a helium balloon on his or her finger and the arm would rise and float. A hypnotic technique related to this phenomenon called ideo-motor signaling pairs an unconscious movement, like the twitch of a particular finger, with a response "Yes" and a different finger connected to the response "No." Then, using a series of yes and no questions, powerful information can be elicited to work on in therapy.

To find the deeper meaning in a patient's life, both Freudian and Jungian psychotherapeutic approaches attempt to interpret the symbolic nature of dreams, although their respective systems are very different. Freudians look at slips of the tongue as revealing of inner truth. Proponents of Behavioral Kinesiology use muscle testing to determine emotional truth. The Labyrinth of Healing is based on the idea that using the tools we have available to us, we can ascertain the deeper truth behind the words of the patient.

Much of the art of psychotherapeutic technique is based on the interpretation of unconscious body language, tone of voice, dreams, slips of the tongue, and repetitive use of phrases, such as 'at this point in time' or 'scared the sh*t out of me.' The therapist looks for congruence between behavior and words. When there is inconsistency, the therapist notes it and looks for a pattern reflecting an idiosyncratic symbolic language of the patient. The limitation of this approach is that the language is often fragile and may not be transferrable from patient to patient.

One of the major advantages of the Emotional Shifting Process is the amount of additional data available to the psychotherapist. The body therapist is keenly aware of the body reactions (remember Dr. McCoy's bed in Star Trek's sick bay), such as, breathing patterns, muscle tension, the pumping of cerebrospinal fluid in the craniosacral system, and even electrical or energetic exchanges in the body.

We are not looking for a truth or lie detector. What we wish to do is target the emotional information or experience that is most relevant to the issue at hand. I refer to this process as the Information Detector (I.D.)

The Information Detector (I.D.) can be thought of as powerful radar to determine what material is most likely to result in positive change for the patient. This method can be used to create a map of the patient's inner world, guide the flow of the session, determine the emotional veracity of the patient's report, and assess the depth of changes in the patient's inner world.

Hal, The Veteran with a Life of Post Traumatic Stress

Hal is a handsome, physically fit, young man whose life fell apart due to Post Traumatic Stress Disorder (PTSD) that followed him out of Afghanistan and his time as an Army Ranger there. He related to me as if he was still in the Army and I, his commanding officer. He presented with every symptom in the diagnostic criteria for PTSD, including vivid flashbacks and nightmares, as if he were reliving the events of the war.

He could not drive in our home town of Sarasota, as drivers dart in and out of traffic. When cars cut in front of him, it reminded him of how the IED (Improvised Explosive Device) was delivered by a man driving a car who snuck in between the trucks in his convoy, and blew up the trucks ahead of him, causing panic. He was hyper-vigilant, always scanning for terrorists in the mall. All in all, he lived in a world of anxiety and depression, couldn't hold a job or a relationship, and was convinced that he would die young.

Hal agreed to participate in the Emotional Shifting Process and commenced a session with Carol Martin and I. The reliving of the attack on his convoy was dramatic and powerful. There were four trucks with Hal riding in the last one. He saw an SUV dart in between the first and second truck of the convoy. He immediately grabbed the phone and tried to warn his comrades, but watched in horror as he saw the car explode, taking with it the first two trucks, his commanding officer and several of his friends. He cried with bitter tears that he had been too late. He recalled the incident with overwhelming emotion. His body moved profoundly, as if he had been storing the blast of the IED in his body and was finally letting go of it. While his improvement was notable, he still suffered from many of his symptoms.

In subsequent sessions, we talked about other traumas from his experience in Afghanistan, but they were not at the core of where he was holding the emotional energy. When I asked him to take a look at his childhood, Carol Martin indicated that his body was resonating with a time around age six. I asked him to tell me about his life at that time. It was as though he was already living in a war zone.

One day, his father, an abusive, raging alcoholic, was beating his mother and siblings. Young Hal jumped on his father's back to try to stop him. His father, infuriated, picked him up and threw him through a plate glass window onto the front lawn. Hal had the sensation of light. He saw an angel who told him that everything was going to be alright. Soon thereafter, he was sent away from his family and raised in a series of foster and boys homes. The impact of the bomb going off in Afghanistan was reminiscent of that early trauma. He had blocked out the memory until our session. The body gave us the information we needed in order to work in an efficient and safe manner.

Following this revelation, Hal began to improve. His paranoia about malls and driving decreased dramatically. He was then able to function at a significantly higher level. Finding the connection between the childhood memory of trauma and his wartime experience was the key to releasing this man from the inner terror that had been unleashed during his military service in Afghanistan.

The Emotional Shifting Process works to disrupt the patterns that cause emotional pain. The re-experiencing of trauma in a supportive atmosphere, along with facilitating a physical release of emotion is an emotionally corrective experience. As the patient opens emotionally, often, he or she is very receptive to learning psychological information that will be helpful in living a productive and happy life. The use of trauma release techniques, such as eye movement, tapping, and breathing, along with simply telling the story, have great healing potential. In the end, we find the meaning the patient placed on the experience underneath the symptom. The path of release and redemption is the most important factor in the process.

4. TRANCE AND MEMORY

"Between the conscious and the unconscious,
the mind has put up a swing: all earth creatures,
even the supernovas, sway between these two trees,
and it never winds down."
–Kabir

"Forbidden to remember, terrified to forget;
it was a hard line to walk."
–Stephenie Meyer, New Moon

Memory is the encoding, storage, and retrieval of information. All psychotherapies, no matter what their philosophy or perspective, whether conventional or radical, will work with memories that have formed patterns of experience, interaction, and behavior. Without memory, learning would be impossible.

Memory involves an interaction among perception, attention, and learning. It influences these processes while also being a result of them. The act of remembering starts with attending to outer events and creating a mental representation. Repetition will result in stronger learning. Long-term memory involves the recall of learned skills; like learning to play a musical instrument or the remembrance of specific experiences. For a memory to move from short term to long-term memory, there must be a passage of time whereby the material is integrated.

Freud identified the idea of repression as a defense against anxiety. Many survivors of trauma report they cannot remember details of an event. Legendary Shaman's have a ritual wherein they journey into the underworld, are metaphorically dismembered, to then have new limbs put on their bodies. In essence, they re-member. We assist patients in recovering lost parts of themselves, and literally, remembering.

Psychology has long known about the Law of State Dependent Learning and Memory. Put simply, the psychophysiological state an individual is in when he or she learns something determines the depth of retrieval of what was learned. If you have been studying for an exam and drank a lot of coffee to stay awake, you'll likely find that you are better able to recall the information if you drink some coffee during the test.

Under conditions of high stress, people spontaneously go into what appear to be trance states. Traumatic experience is encoded into memory in that manner. Reports of individuals who have been through traumatic events sound similar to hypnotic phenomena. Time either speeds up or slows down, individuals may have hazy or highly focused awareness, and emotions will be either be isolated or overwhelming. Therefore, recollection of traumatic events is often best facilitated in a similar state (trance) to the one in which the memory was created.

Many psychotherapists shun hypnosis. Nevertheless, hypnotic phenomena can teach us a great deal about healing. The trance state elicited by hypnosis is a natural and normal state of consciousness. The sensation of being in a hypnotic state feels like daydreaming, relaxing, or being fully absorbed in a creative activity. Hypnotherapy's power resides in its capacity to engage the subconscious, that critically important part of the mind that must be tapped for true healing to occur.

Why is the subconscious so important? Consider this: most people consciously desire health, wealth, and love. Yet many behave in ways that seem calculated to thwart, rather than realize these desires. Why? Because the conscious mind is not the sole determinant of behavior. If it were, the world would contain healthier, wealthier, and more emotionally fulfilled inhabitants.

Milton Erickson, the great American psychiatrist, addressed this dichotomy. I often borrow Erickson's metaphor of the conscious mind being the front of the mind, while the subconscious mind, the back of it. For deep psychological change to take place, direct communication with the back of the mind must occur. Experience has shown me the patient's subconscious mind often knows more than either the therapist or the patient. In fact, once accessed, the subconscious provides all the symbols and metaphors needed to change, and ultimately heal.

In graduate school, I was amazed and disappointed to find not a single course in hypnosis, and only one brief mention of it in a class on behavior therapy. I decided to learn the rudiments of this technique outside school. I found hypnosis is merely a specific, conscious state of focused attention, easily attained by most people. Individuals go in and out of trance all day long, although they do not usually notice. For example, if you drive to work the same way every day, spend the drive thinking about something else, and not really focused on driving, or if you get very absorbed in books, music, or movies and don't notice the passage of time, you are likely in a trance state.

The psyche is naturally set up for health and healing. Trance, as a psycho-physiological state, regardless of the methods used to access it, is critical to consider due to it's ability to engage states of consciousness that have the best chance to facilitate healing.

Maria, The 10 Year Old Cancer Survivor

One of my first experiences utilizing trance in healing happened while working at a children's cancer clinic. Maria, a beautiful, ten-year old child, was diagnosed with childhood leukemia. When I met her, she was wearing a bandanna on her head to hide the fact that most of her hair had been lost due to chemotherapy. She was having acute anxiety reactions to the chemo. The youngster would become nauseous on her way to the hospital, and her parents found it increasingly difficult to motivate her to accept treatment for her illness. Her sparkling, bright blue eyes lit up with the idea that we were going to work on solving the problem.

Children are naturals at accessing their inner world of imagination, and Maria was a stellar performer. She was able to easily access a deeply relaxed, highly imaginative state of trance. Once there, I asked her what it was that made her sick to her stomach. She replied, "I hate the smell of chemotherapy. I smell it all the time, but it really gets out of control on the way to the hospital." "What is a scent or aroma you would like to smell instead of the chemo?" I asked her. I was expecting her to respond with roses or some other pleasant fragrance, but this child was certainly more brilliant than I. She hesitated for a moment, and then with a big smile on her face, she said "Gasoline." I encouraged Maria to imagine her mother pulling into a gas station to fill up the car. The expression on her face changed instantly to that of someone who was indeed inhaling something strong, and then almost simultaneously, both happy and victorious, "I can smell it, I can really smell the gasoline." She cried out.

After that, her parents had few problems with her coming to the unit for treatment. The change in her behavior was apparent to staff, as well as her mother, and persisted through the remaining months of treatment.

Tammy Cannot Swallow

My work with eating disorder patients provided another venue to use trance phenomena in the service of healing. Tammy, a 42-year-old woman I met while working on an inpatient eating disorders unit was dangerously underweight and malnourished. She was different from patients with anorexia nervosa in that she wanted to gain weight, but had tremendous difficulty swallowing. None of her physicians had been able to find a structural or physiological cause for her symptoms. I was asked by her psychiatrist to use regression hypnosis with her. In the first session, with the psychiatrist present, I suggested she take herself to what she was having difficulty swallowing.

Speaking from trance, she recounted difficulties endured in her childhood at the hands of her abusive father. Tammy was forbidden to express herself and figuratively swallowed her feelings. She released a considerable amount of emotion, and responded to my suggestion that when she came out of trance, her throat would feel dry and she would be able to swallow deeply. When she complied, the psychiatrist registered a very odd expression on his face, as though he could not believe his eyes.

After completion of the session, I went into the nurse's station to write notes. About ten minutes later, the psychiatrist burst into the room to breathlessly tell me the patient was extremely anxious and had broken out in a skin rash. I immediately returned to the treatment room with the psychiatrist and patient, where the patient rapidly went back into trance. I then asked if there was anything else she was unable to swallow. She talked about her husband's alcoholism, a circumstance she had neglected to mention at the intake interview. While she was addressing this subject, her rash cleared up before our eyes. I then gave her the suggestion that soon she would find herself eating a cracker. The staff later reported this did occur shortly after the session ended.

Tammy's general mental and physical health improved while in the hospital, as her discomfort at swallowing improved markedly. However, she still had to address the harsh reality of a marriage that was very painful.

Donna Binge Eats Chocolate

My training and experience in Psychodrama opened a door regarding the potential for the use of trance in therapy. Donna, a 39 year old nurse, attended a group therapy for people experiencing psycho-spiritual events. Donna related that she had a problem with binge eating chocolate that started during childhood, when she would sneak Baker's chocolate from her stepmother's kitchen. One of the activities patients in this group participated in was a psychodrama technique known as family sculpting. This technique required the primary player choose group members to take on the roles of individuals acting as if they were in his or her family of origin. The actors are then placed in time, space, and position, with each one of them being given something important to say.

Donna gave her "stepmother" the statement, "If you screw up one more time, you are going to be sent to Baker's School." Donna explained that Baker's school was a reform school in her hometown. As the "actors" began to speak their individual statements, Donna had an odd reaction. Every time the actor protraying her stepmother spoke the statement about Baker's School aloud, Donna would drop into what looked like a deep trance, eyes closed, breathing slowed, with limp body posture, then quickly pop out of it when the next actor said her statement. I was alerted to this by one of the actors, who exclaimed, "What is happening to Donna?" We all seemed to make the connection at the same time. One of the group members became very excited and started to speak directly to Donna. "Do you see it, that's the binge eating, Baker's school and Baker's chocolate," she cried out. Donna had no awareness of this, but asked if I would use hypnosis to work on this issue.

Donna was a wonderful hypnotic subject and went into deep trance quickly and easily. She indicated she wished to erase the tape that had the chocolate binge eating on it. She acknowledged this was connected to her fear that her stepmother would send her away. She ate to reduce her fear that she would be abandoned. After the session, she had the first significant respite from binge eating that she had experienced in years.

Sal's Time Distortion

The relationship between trance and high stress was evidenced by Sal's experience in a car accident. Sal, a 20-year-old college student, was stopped at a traffic light. While waiting for the light to change, a car plowed into him from behind. Sal didn't think he was hurt initially, but about 24 hours later, his neck began to feel stiff and painful. He went for massage therapy, but relief was only temporary. His massage therapist referred him to me.

During our first meeting, Sal said, "I remember thinking to myself, 'I guess the guy in the car behind me must have realized he was going to hit me. I heard screeching of brakes, but then the oddest thing happened. I began to see things in a series of snapshots, maybe one every second or so. I couldn't figure out why my head was getting so close to the windshield of my car. It felt like time was moving really slowly. Then I guess the seat belt must have grabbed me just before I hit the glass. I was pulled back into real time. I heard glass breaking and metal twisting from the impact. What should have taken a split second felt like it took ten or fifteen seconds."

I realized Sal had experienced a time distortion effect one often finds in trance phenomena. He must have gone into a very deep trance state during the trauma and would not be able to release the emotion stored using conventional therapy. He needed something deeper.

Carol Martin helped unlock this experience for Sal using the Emotional Shifting Process. While he lay on the table, with Carol lightly touching his shoulder, I helped Sal easily access a trance state. Sal rapidly connected with the fear and anger he had suppressed during the accident. During the session, he realized he felt he might be terribly hurt and expressed his anger at the carelessness of the other driver, something he had not felt during the accident. This was key in releasing energy stored in his neck that was causing him pain. Soon thereafter, Sal's conventional therapies began to work and he recovered.

One of the goals of the Emotional Shifting Process is to work with the emotion attached to memory. Memories with emotion linked to them are called 'active memories.' Memories without an emotional charge are called 'passive memories.' If you recall what you had for breakfast, as you visualize your coffee or toast, likely there is little to no emotion connected with it. This is a passive memory. However, remembering a recent traumatic event, such as a car accident, you may feel emotional, as well as a little foggy. This is an active memory. The memory or learning of that situation are encoded in the non-ordinary state. Included in that state are the emotions, whether experienced consciously or unconsciously at the time. Therefore, in order to work with the pattern created by trauma, we must access states similar to those existing at the time of the trauma.

The strength of the encoding of emotional material is determined by how it impacts the psyche or it's salience. Salience, in emotional memory patterns, may be created either by events of low energy or emotion, but high frequency, high energy or emotion with low frequency, or catastrophic one time learning. We have encountered all three types of memory encoding while using the Emotional Shifting Process.

Aaron's Stomach Distress

An example of an event with low energy, but high frequency was the case of Aaron. Aaron, a 34 year old, practicing attorney, had unexplained stomach problems.

He agreed to use the Emotional Shifting Process, as his symptoms did not resolve under his physician's treatment. The Information Detector indicated that the point of origin of the problem was age eight, that it connected to his relationship with his father, but it seemed to last over a long period of time. When I asked him what he most remembered about his father, he sighed, and said, "Dad was the worst insomniac I've ever known. We had to be incredibly quiet during the evening on the chance that he might fall asleep." Aaron expressed that this had been a constant worry throughout his adolescence. As we worked on it, his gut relaxed. Over several sessions, he saw his stomach problems ease.

Margaret Has the World On Her Shoulders

A case of a high energy, low frequency events, was that of Margaret, a professional golfer on the Ladies PGA. Margaret's father was also her coach. He had an extreme temper, activated most acutely if she did not put his coaching into practice immediately. She was always waiting for him to blow up. The pressure on her to succeed was intense, affecting her game, and her life. She began to have shoulder pain, which resisted healing regardless of what her physical therapist tried. She agreed to work with the Emotional Shifting Process.

In the first session, the I.D. indicated there was a strong emotional component to her pain. I asked her what I believed to be an obvious question given her symptoms. "Margaret," I intoned. "What is on your shoulders?"

She sighed deeply and then related the pressure put on her by her father. She felt she was carrying the family on her shoulders, both emotionally and financially. She began to release her feelings. About a week later, she called to tell me the physical therapy was starting to show good results.

Roger Has No Memory

An example of catastrophic, one trial learning is the case of Roger. Roger, a 38 year old, married man, reported that he had no personal memory. He knew how to use a fork and knife, and could do all the things that most people do, but had complete amnesia about his own life.

Roger was found unconscious at a rest stop in northern Florida in his work van. When he awakened, he was very confused and disoriented. When his family met him at the hospital, he did not recognize his wife and children. He had no memory of his life history or his job.

He had been given an extensive neurological workup with negative results. He had some hypnosis, but made no progress. He came in to my office with his wife who was very upset about the situation. Roger was oddly peaceful about it. After all, he related, his wife was pretty and the kids were cute, so why worry?

To please his wife more than anything else, Roger agreed to use the Emotional Shifting Process. The first two sessions did not yield any new memories for Roger, but gave us important information. His body resonated strongly with the idea there was a trauma he was not yet ready to remember.

Near the end of the third session, I encouraged him to go into a deeper state, and gave him a suggestion that he would remember one thing from the trauma, then quickly forget it. He opened his eyes, and said, "Hey, there are guys in my van." Then he seemed to stop, his eyes misted over and he changed the subject.

During the next session, I felt we were ready to

open the memories up significantly. Carol Martin indicated that his body resonated with the idea that it was time to recover the memories. I encouraged a relaxed state once again, and said simply, "Is the body ready to give Roger his memories back." Carol nodded her head, "Yes."

I said, "Okay, I'm going to count to three. You will open your eyes and reclaim your memories. One, Two, Three." He sat up from the massage table. He looked up at the diplomas on my office wall. He said, "Binghamton, I was once in Binghamton," then his eyes filled with tears as his memories came flooding back. I ran out to the waiting room and returned with his wife. He leapt off the table to hug her in powerful recognition.

Once they had a chance to connect, I asked if he remembered what happened in the van. He said, "Yes, I stopped in the middle of the night. I was too tired to drive anymore and thought I might crash the car. I was awakened by four guys with guns, who told me they were going to kill me if I didn't give them money and all the goods in the van. I guess I didn't move quickly enough because one of the men pistol-whipped me, another put his gun in my face, but it misfired. Just at that moment another car drove up and the guys fled, but not before hitting me again with the pistol and knocking me out. That was the last I remembered until now. Now I know what happened." Roger was able to reconnect with his wife and children, and went back to work soon thereafter.

The Emotional Shifting Process works to disrupt the patterns that cause emotional pain. The re-experiencing of traumatic memory in a supportive atmosphere, the resonating psycho-physiological state (trance), along with facilitating a physical release of energy is an emotionally corrective experience. As the patients open, they are more receptive to learning psychological information that will enhance their lives.

5. BIRTH

*Each birth connects lives from
beginningless time and boundless space.*
–Gems of Tibetan Wisdom

Being present at the births of my children remains the two greatest experiences of my life. Placing my hands under the tiny armpits of my younger son, and guiding him out of the birth canal, I felt the ecstasy of new life and the privilege of being the first to greet Daniel as he entered the world. My older boy, Jonathan was born via Cesarean Section. Although he was delivered behind a curtain, obscuring the procedure from my vision, I was present inside the surgical theatre. Immediately prior to this procedure, his mother had been given sedatives to help calm her, and she drifted off into a peaceful sleeplike state. The newborn did not initially cry when removed from his mother's womb, but once the nurse began to clean him up, he began crying and then howling with considerable gusto. The nurse, realizing the child's mother was unavailable, placed him in my arms.

As I felt the first touch of his tiny body, powerful feelings ignited within me. I began to simultaneously laugh and cry. For the next thirty minutes, I found myself strangely alternating between these two emotional responses. However, throughout my venting of emotional expression, the infant had been quiet, his tiny form having molded to my body much in the manner of a warm blanket. It was one of the most startling and elevating experiences of my life. Several days later, I recalled the circumstances and mused to Dr. Lawrence Ricker, one of my psychotherapy professors at the University of South Florida, "It was as if ancient tapes had been played inside of me." My older son's birth was a foreshadowing of events that would change the way I thought about human consciousness and the practice of psychotherapy

Modern science is beginning to corroborate what many millions of mothers have known for centuries: the quality of intrauterine life and the birth experience itself exert a significant impact on the health and welfare of human life. The results of studies regarding the emotional ramifications of the intrauterine world, suggest the fetus possesses consciousness. The events in the womb, and during birth, have identifiable, as well as, residual effects on emotional and behavioral functioning.

Fetuses are capable of rudimentary learning in utero. An example of this can be found in the work of James DeCasper, who taught sixteen pregnant women to read aloud the Dr. Seuss story "The Cat in the Hat" while employing a particular cadence for the benefit of their fetuses. These mothers-to-be read the story twice a day during the final six weeks of their pregnancy. Then, after birth, the babies were given a choice of two pacifiers, each connected to an audiotape player.

Remarkably, all babies tested in the study exhibited a pronounced preference for the pacifier connected to the familiar voice, thus implying they both remembered it, and were attracted to the cadence they had previously heard from their mothers. Moreover, additional studies determined newborns selected lullabies sung to them while in utero from those which they were unfamiliar with, They were partial to their mother's voice over other voices, and even demonstrate a propensity for the language heard the mother speak during the pregnancy.

Studies examining the information gleaned from subjects undergoing regression hypnosis to access intrauterine or birth events have provided surprisingly strong evidence the data recorded during these sessions may be reliable and valid. David Cheek, MD, the late obstetrician and accomplished hypnotist, utilized notes locked in his files for more than twenty years regarding births he had attended, comparing them with behaviors exhibited under hypnotic trance by these same individuals as adults. Cheek found each of his ten subjects had closely reproduced almost the exact movements of the head and shoulders the physician had noted at the time of birth.

Even in the most routine of instances, birth can be seen as a heroic journey. Although the birth canal is usually only three to four inches in length, the infant has no knowledge of this. The infant begins to leaves the insulated and protected environment of the womb and enters a storm of unknown duration and intensity. During contractions, the uterine muscles may constrict from multiple directions simultaneously, the experience of which is unlikely to provide reassurance for the tiny traveler.

At the height of labor, the exertion of the uterus may produce forces upwards of fifty to one hundred pounds that impact the body of the infant. During the most powerful of uterine contractions, the infant may be isolated from communication, nutritional sustenance, and even oxygen. In addition, the mother's verbal, emotional, and physical reactions to the pain associated with labor and birth are generally heightened and may be imparted to the infant.

When birth is traumatic, the encounter that results can be a tumultuous struggle against primordial forces and impressive odds. Psychologist David Chamberlain asserted the infant may endure near-death experiences during this time, as he or she moves through dynamic and dramatic physical, emotional, and spiritual energies. Dr. Chamberlain documented the concept that infants experience pain and may contend with considerable suffering during the process of labor and birth. He believes any traumatic event impacting the infant during intrauterine life has potential to be encoded on the cells of the developing fetus and affect the individual at a later time.

Chamberlain added valuable research evidence pertaining to the importance, validity, and reliability of birth memories. He systematically compared the birth memories of ten independently hypnotized mother-child pairs. All of the mothers in the study stated they had never revealed details of birth to their children prior to the study and none of the children reported any previous birth memories. He reported, "The content of birth memories suggests a sophisticated level of physical, mental, and emotional consciousness at birth, beyond anything predicted by developmental psychology."

When working with the possible effects of such early experiences, ascertaining and verifying the accuracy of the reports, is, to say the least, difficult. I encourage patients to utilize what they already consciously know about their intrauterine life and birth and integrate this information with what they imagine those experiences would be like. We receive strong indications through the Information Detector, (I.D.) whether or not the patient is working on emotionally significant material.

Conception can be seen as a miraculous, alchemical event in which the sperm and egg, cells without the potential to produce anything alone, combine with each other in a glorious rendezvous to create the DNA matrix of a human being. If we consider the idea that both mother and father may have unconscious awareness of this event, conception can be viewed as a metaphor for their future interactions with their child. Taking this idea forward, the thoughts, feelings, and attitudes of both parents are imagined as encoded in that first cell at the instant of its genesis. As the individual grows, cells are copied from the initial cell, and the events of conception are potentially copied onto every cell of that person.

Since there is no known scientific means of pinpointing the instant of conception, when conception is indicated as the point of origin of an emotional issue, I encourage the patient to use all he or she knows about the circumstances of his or her parent's lives around that time period. This includes conscious knowledge regarding the parent's attitudes about children, among a host of other relevant material. I also engage the imagination of the patient in an effort to uncover and create a metaphor that expresses the emotional energies associated with his or her conception.

At times, intrauterine events are considered significant by the subconscious mind. When this is the case, I generally ask the patient to imagine traveling up the umbilical cord for the purpose of connecting with mother's central nervous system to determine her emotional state.

Implantation of the blastocyst into the uterine lining also has the potential to be an emotionally significant event. The developing fetus must physically adhere to his or her mother's body and begin to be nourished by her in order to survive. This initial mother-child connection may also ignite an emotional interaction of great metaphorical and symbolic power.

The point at which mother consciously discovers she is pregnant may also be an important emotional moment for the mother, the fetus, and the future relationship. Parental reactions have the potential to flow down from the mother through the placenta and umbilical cord and affect the developing fetus. I suggest to the patient that he or she can either experience emotion moving through his or her own body, or to project awareness into mother's central nervous system in an attempt to access information.

Paul's Difficult Birth: Cord Around His Neck

Paul was a lanky, good-looking, sixteen-year-old. He was bright, alert, and intense. His mother, Anne, a nurse, brought him to me after he repeatedly refused to share any household chores or even to begin homework assignments. He tended to isolate, was losing weight, and seemed depressed. Conventional therapy had not changed things for Paul.

Paul had a number of excuses to explain his unwillingness to cooperate. However, even his intelligent mind could not provide adequate explanation for his refusal to perform tasks rewarded by privileges or money. I thought the teenager might benefit from the Emotional Shifting Process. Anne readily agreed. Physical Therapist, Grace Walters worked with me on Paul.

When he and his mother arrived, the boy expressed strong reservations about the unfamiliar type of therapy, but his sparkling eyes and pointed humor provided evidence that he was intrigued regarding what might transpire. "I am here under protest," his tone was self-righteous, "but I'll do it for Mom."

I asked Paul if he wanted his mother present during the session and he said no. As he lay on his back on the therapeutic table, I began to chat with Paul while Grace connected with him by placing her hands lightly on his head. Almost instantaneously, the boy began to stir and then to writhe until he had coiled his body into what can most accurately be described as a fetal position. This was a good place to begin.

Paul shifted his body position and practically launched himself off the therapeutic table. We scrambled to catch him and managed to lower him gently to the ground. Once Paul was situated, Grace whispered to me that the patient's trip from the table to the floor might connect to a birth experience. I suggested to Paul that he tell us what he knew and thought about birth. "I think birth would be scary," he replied.

I encouraged him to imagine he was in back in his mother's womb. I explained to him the two ways he could be born: to move normally down the birth canal or to be surgically removed from the uterus by means of a caesarian section. Since his mother was in the waiting room, I used this opportunity to ask her directly regarding details regarding Paul's birth. Grace cradled Paul's head in her arms as I went outside briefly to speak with his mother.

Anne reported that after twenty-two hours of labor, Paul became stuck for several hours in the birth canal. Up to that time, his birth had been proceeding normally. She told me the delivery was complicated by his head being upside down. She had a strong feeling that the umbilical cord was wrapped around his head and neck. Her eyes misted momentarily when she said that Paul had to be delivered surgically.

Back in my office, I found Paul lying contorted on the floor with Grace by his side. I lay down next to him, placing my head by his. I suggested he look for the baby he once was. I paused, and then inquired,

"Paul, did you find him yet?" "Yeah," he replied. "What's going on?" I continued.

The bravado and wit he exhibited at the beginning of the session were gone, replaced by a small shaky vocalization. "I don't think this baby can come out." "Why not?" I pressed. Paul became more animated. "It's the cord," he said excitedly. "I don't think the baby can untangle the cord." "How does this baby feel about being tangled in the cord?" I inquired.

Paul's breathing perceptibly shifted as he reacted to my query. His emotions were beginning to shut down. "I'm not sure," he replied in a clipped tone. "Paul," I said, "you sound frustrated." "I suppose so," he replied icily. I confronted him more strongly. "How about a lot frustrated?" His breathing increased, and his body tensed appreciably. "Yeah," he countered, "a lot frustrated. This baby is angry." He snarled at me. "How angry?" I continued. Paul glowered at me. "This baby is furious!" Countering his anger with calmness, I spoke in a very thoughtful voice. "Paul, what does this baby do when he is furious."

He refused to respond. I gently explained to Paul that his silence and body rigidity were nonverbal expressions of anger. For Paul, the cutting-off of his emotions in response to frustration as a baby paralleled his behavior when challenged by any obstruction later in life. When he became angry, he wouldn't do his homework, he avoided chores, starved himself, and isolated from his friends, shutting down just like the baby. Grace whispered to me her impression that due to the increased muscle tension in his body, Paul was ready to release the emotions he had been holding.

I encouraged Paul to help the baby untangle the umbilical cord. As he did so, he visibly relaxed. I gave him the choice regarding his wish to have a surgical birth or a normal birth. Paul chose to journey down the birth canal and be born naturally.

Grace huddled close to Paul on the floor, forming a makeshift birth canal. She began to push against him, imitating his mother's contractions during labor. I suggested he work his way out of the womb, To that end, Grace restrained him from easy movement thorough the "birth canal." He pushed with considerable strength against us, and as he reached the end of the tunnel, I moved back and received him as he emerged. We stood up and, with Grace at our side, went out to see his mother, who had been nearby in my waiting room. I announced to her, "Anne, you have a beautiful baby boy," and guided him into her arms.

He lay there blissfully, smiling widely, his long thin legs hanging over the edge of the chair. His mother took the time to bond with him and told him how much she loved him.

Now possessing a clearer understanding of his indirect expression of anger, Paul continued to see me for psychotherapy. Anne reported that her son's school performance improved and he was generally more cooperative at home. Anne glowed, describing the improvement in Paul's confidence level. "He can now complete the things he starts," she said. This was certainly fitting for an individual who had rewritten the script of his own birth and completed the biological process of traveling down the birth canal.

Preston: Not My Day, Not My Way

Another potential area of emotional trauma can be seen in patients who were born via C-section or induced labor. Here is a case of an evolved individual who felt stuck and got relief from examining his birth issues. Preston, a physician from Virginia, spent an entire week with us working intensively to resolve his acknowledged insecurities. His girlfriend had suggested he inquire of me regarding the possible origin of a persistent tickle in his throat. I sensed this might indeed be the logical place to begin our work. Massage therapist, Carol Martin, agreed to assist using the Emotional Shifting Process.

Preston lay on the therapeutic table as Carol tuned in to the energies of his body. I began to speak with him about taking a tour of his life. We went back through his training, his college and high school days, and then through his childhood. I.D. indicated Preston's body resonated with a point in time during labor, just prior to his birth. As soon as this was mentioned to Preston, he blurted out angrily, "I can taste the chemicals they are using to induce me. The doctor did it because he wanted to go out of town for the weekend and didn't want to wait for me." I thought it ironic a trained physician would openly communicate such an indictment of a colleague.

Preston appeared to access his mother's anger with the situation. As he did so, he pursed his lips in fury. "Not my day, not my way," he raged, repeating the words over and over, in a voice increasingly loud and defiant. Though the thought occurred to me, albeit fleetingly, to encourage Preston to explore his anger even more deeply, I sensed he was deriving comfort from blaming others for his misfortune. With this in mind, I very gently directed him to get in touch with the higher part of himself to discover why he had chosen to have experienced this kind of birth. He paused and turned inward. After a few moments, he started to sob.

"Not only was it my day, but it was my way," he whispered, barely audibly. Preston had realized that he needed to experience the pain associated with the induced birth. That experience propelled him to develop the motivation and resolve to transcend conventional allopathic medicine. He eventually transitioned his practice to focus on holistic medicine. He became the type of physician who would look more extensively for natural solutions in his own practice of the healing arts.

Slipping into a deeper trance, he indicated he was experiencing his mother birthing him naturally this time. After a brief period of modest discomfort, he began to release the emotional energies he had retained at the time of his initial birth trauma. Having allowed his body to enact a chemical-free birth sequence, he spontaneously began to "migrate" off the therapeutic table. With assistance from Carol and myself, he was lowered safely to the floor.

A few moments later Preston spoke without prompting about the nurturing aspects of his relationship with his mother. He acknowledged she had sacrificed her own comfort to make possible the experience of his painful, chemically induced birth. He sobbed, comprehending the discomfort had been shared. He had the awareness that his experience facilitated a significant professional direction for his life. A few weeks later Preston called to report his self-assurance had improved tremendously following his therapeutic work. He had become more open with medical colleagues regarding his use of alternative medicine. As he did, the success of his practice grew. For these two patients, re-experiencing and releasing the energy of the place where they were stuck during birth resulted in powerful healing experiences.

Dorothy: Car Wreck In The Womb

A most dramatic story documenting the emotional ramifications of a traumatic experience during intrauterine life was that of Dorothy, a thirty-two-year-old former nurse who was attending acupuncture school. Dorothy came to me for treatment of anxiety. During the initial interview, she told me about lifelong embarassment from a scar located on her chin. For Dorothy, this was a physical reminder of a series of surgeries she endured to correct a birth defect. Massage Therapist Carol Martin assisted me with Dorothy.

I.D. indicated the origin of Dorothy's anxiety was eight months into her development as a fetus. When she heard this, Dorothy grew anxious. I suggested she move her awareness up the umbilical cord in an effort to ascertain if something had happened to her mother. She said, "Mom is scared. We were moving fast. I feel like we stopped suddenly." Her speech then became pressured. "My body seemed to fly through the womb and crashed into something hard," she insisted. "My chin was crushed by the impact." Then Dorothy's voice then reduced to a whisper. "Someone died. I see a little boy." At the beginning of our second session, Dorothy excitedly related that she asked her mother if anything unusual happened in the latter stages of her pregnancy. "Mom was avoiding something," she related, "and although I tried to be insistent, she refused to comment and quickly changed the subject."

Undaunted, Dorothy contacted another family member, who informed her that her mother was involved in a serious car accident when she was eight months pregnant. A seven-year-old boy riding in the other vehicle had been killed. Dorothy's uncannily accurate perception and memory of an event that occurred in utero proved to validate and heal her. She had created a powerful context to understand herself, while also releasing fears and insecurities that had plagued her throughout life.

John: Death Lingers In The Womb

The final case history in this chapter is that of John. John, a married, forty-one-year-old physician with four beautiful children, began to suffer from severe anxiety approximately two years prior to our first meeting. Analytical, he speculated his anxiety had been initiated by a decidedly negative interaction with his mother. He indicated interest in the Emotional Shifting Process when the topic came up in therapy. Massage Therapist Carol Martin worked with me on John.

We began the initial session talking about John's relationship with his mother. John shared that he and his mother had never gotten along very well.

He spoke of conflict with her throughout his life. As we moved back through his life experiences the I.D. pointed us towards his pre-natal life and then his conception. Since we cannot document with any certainty a "memory" of conception, I suggested John think of it as an imprinting of emotion on the first cell. I asked him to speculate about his parent's feelings at the time he was conceived. Almost instantly, he was struck by images of his mother and father exhibiting intense fear. He revealed both of his parents held the fear the new baby would turn out to be malformed.

I suggested to John that he explore the conditions of his implantation in his mother's uterine wall. As he did so, the patient indicated he felt as if "winds of fear" emanated from his mother, which made uniting with her difficult. He had the realization he would die if he did not secure the attachment to his mother. John related that he propelled himself toward the wall and hurled himself against it. He described himself crashing into the uterine wall, literally "hanging on for dear life" as the energized forces of mother's fear made his perch most precarious and threatened to repel him.

After he weathered this "storm," I encouraged him to reveal details surrounding his mother's conscious discovery of her own pregnancy. In so doing, he reported sensing a powerful combination of love and fear. Then, unexpectedly, he began to cry. "She's worried I'll die like my older sister did. She died in childbirth." John then described how his sister died during delivery as a result of a prolapsed umbilical cord. "My mother knew something was wrong and called the doctor." John took a deep breath, sighed, and then continued. "The doctor told her that nothing was wrong. By the time she finally got to the hospital, the baby was dead."

While John was aware of an older sister, he had never felt any emotion regarding her demise. John revealed that in his mother's womb he could feel the energy of his sister's death still residing there. Despite the fear this generated, he continued to develop, progressing right up to the onset of labor. As he allowed himself this experience, he related not only his anxiety regarding the process, but also his sense of guilt from knowing he might survive when his sister had not.

John reported being very tense as he pushed his way down the birth passage. His response to the increasing pain was violent anger. As he writhed on the therapeutic table, his face had become a crimson mask, and he was drenched in perspiration. Then, from somewhere deep within, he grunted, "I can survive. I will survive." John's long, loud moan seemed to express more longing than fear. "I can see my sister's spirit!" he cried out. "She is guiding me down the birth canal." His tears flowed freely as he choked out his words. "She is forming a link between my mother and the baby that is me." He sobbed, then his emotion eased. "She is calming both of us, so we can finally release her."

John ceased speaking as his body mimicked the myriad movements associated with birth. I prepared myself for his rolling off the table by placing my knees on the floor by the table's edge and bracing my back. I was able to catch him and slowly lowered him to the floor, while Carol carefully arranged blankets around him. John's left shoulder, the one that had given him pain for almost ten years, began to move involuntarily. As Carol gently facilitated that movement, John reported he felt a sharp pain in his shoulder, followed quickly by the feeling of warmth flowing through it.

Spontaneously he recounted how shortly after birth, he had been placed in a bassinet. Very uncomfortable, he began searching frantically for his mother's breast. Using this as a cue, I grabbed a pillow and placed it under his head. He snuggled against it and relaxed noticeably. Soon John presented a most peaceful countenance. Though his eyes darted about under their closed lids in what appeared to be a waking dream state, he seemed both comfortable and comforted.

When John returned for his next session he enthusiastically announced he had telephoned his mother and inquired about some of the specifics surrounding his birth. Her response greatly surprised him. "John," she had informed him with a deep sigh, "we sure had a bad time with that shoulder of yours, the doctor had to dislocate it." He further indicated that his shoulder had been symptom free since his last session, even under the pressure of a rigorous athletic regimen. He wrote me a note about a year later to confirm that neither his anxiety, nor his pain had returned.

The birth process, intrauterine life, and even conception provide powerful metaphors for emotional healing. I am supportive of whatever will help the seeker as he or she journies through the Labyrinth, to the core, and then out again.

6. CHILDREN

*"May what I do flow from me like a river, no forcing
and no holding back, the way it is with children."*
–Rainer Maria Rilke

In my experience as a psychotherapist, I often find patients who are able to reveal pertinent material only when they "present" themselves as if they were very young children. At times, we will be working at a point in a patient's life where defensive strategies and structures were initiated. While these approaches to life may have reduced anxiety and increased a sense of security during childhood, they have the potential to create great difficulty for adult functioning. Consequently, it is very important for the therapist to understand the emotional and cognitive development of the inner child being displayed.

The conversations with these "inner" children are very much the same as those I might have with "real" children. Because of the disparity between the adult's physical presence and the childlike quality of the conversation, special attention is given to the language, images, and symbols being expressed by the patient. Simultaneously, I remain sensitive to the relationships unfolding among the patient, the body therapist, and myself in the moment.

Ricky: My Parents Divorce Was Sh*tty

Actual children are usually very receptive to the Emotional Shifting Process. Ricky was a bright 11 year-old son of a local physician who was exhibiting encopresis (having bowel movements in his pants). His father had referred patients to me in the past, and knew about the Emotional Shifting Process. Massage Therapist, Carol Martin worked with me with this child.

Ricky lay down on the therapeutic table and stared at the ceiling, Carol touched his right shoulder with her hand and we began to dialogue. I asked Ricky if he knew why he was here. He said, "I'm pooping in my pants." I asked him very directly what was the "sh*ttiest" thing that had ever happened in his life. He looked up at me, his eyes filling with tears and quietly said, "My parents divorce." Carol, feeling the I.D. resonate with his words, nodded in agreement. I responded, "Have you told them how upset you are?" "No," he said, "They have enough problems without me." I gently suggested he might feel better if he talked with them.

Carol went out into the waiting room and brought his father into the session. Ricky sat up and told his father how sad and angry he was about the divorce, and then began to cry. His dad held him and they cried together. His father called me a week later to report that the symptom had vanished. We met for a follow up session two weeks later and the symptom had not returned. A one session "fix" is rare, but not unheard of.

Tommy: Bedwetter, Dry As The Desert

In another case, the Emotional Shifting Process helped a child who had a similar embarrassing and debilitating problem. Tommy, a nine-year-old with bright blue eyes and jet-black hair, looked like a child movie star. However, his good looks and engaging personality belied a difficulty, which steadfastly resisted a solution. Tommy was a bed wetter.

Tommy's family made several attempts to overcome the problem. For a few months, he slept with an alarm designed to wake him at the first sign of moisture, and train him to wake himself before he wet the bed. The device, Tommy's father reported, resulted in only one dry night during the entire time it was used. Prescribed medications and several trips to a hypnotist proved no more effective than the moisture alarm. One intervention or another would work for a period of time, but never for very long. By the time his parents brought Tommy to my office, he was wetting the bed almost nightly. The fear of doing so made him dread going to sleep.

As a result of his emotional difficulties, other behavioral problems began to surface. Tommy was having trouble with his schoolwork. He was also withdrawing and isolating himself from even his closest friends. A longstanding problem with nightmares began to intensify. His parents grew increasingly concerned. When his father learned about the Emotional Shifting Process, he contacted me in the hope I might help his son.

As with most of my patients, I began my first session with Tommy in brief conversation before asking him to lie down on the table. Gently, Carol Martin placed her hands underneath his head. I told Tommy I would be talking to him while she "tuned in" to his body. Very softly, I explained to the young patient that there was a front part of his mind and a back part. The front part, I said, was the part that remembered what he had to do for homework or what time his favorite program was on TV. The back part of his mind knew about his hopes and dreams and memories. I told him I believed that the back part of his mind knew how to help him solve his problem and that was the part I wanted to talk to.

Children of Tommy's age usually have little trouble giving their imagination free reign. They can connect with the subconscious mind fairly easily and Tommy was no exception. He slipped into a deep trance state almost immediately. His breathing slowed, his eyes began to move as if he was in dreaming sleep, and his musculature relaxed deeply. Carol indicated that he was ready to begin.

I began a therapeutic dialogue to determine the origin of his presenting problem. As Carol monitored the child's body reactions, sensitive information was being revealed. Her ability to feel the flow of energy and where a blockage exists in a patient's body is impressive. Carol's sensitive connection with Tommy's subtle emotional reactions allowed us to find strong indications that the cause of his problem could be traced to an event that had occurred when he was two years old. This corroborated something Tommy's father had said in a pre-session interview. Apparently, when Tommy was two, his mother had become so depressed following her own mother's death that she was placed in a psychiatric hospital for two months.

As I guided Tommy back to the age of two, Carol carefully monitored the patient's physical reactions to identify places in the child's body that contained pockets of emotional energy. I asked Tommy to tell me what the two-year-old was feeling at the time. He whispered, I'm angry with himself for not taking better care of my mother. As he said this, Carol signaled to me that his body was starting to release energy near the base of the spine and stomach.

Carol indicated that there was also substantial energy stuck in the throat. It occurred to me Tommy needed to cry out for his mother. When I asked him to call out to her, he tried valiantly, but the sound he made was barely audible.

Though we were nearing the end of the session and Tommy had released considerable emotional energy, I felt we had yet to uncover what specifically gave the symptom its power.

The following week, Tommy's father reported that his son had a difficult time in the interval between sessions. In addition to his nightly bedwetting, Tommy had been troubled by severe nightmares, in addition to generalized, unrelenting fear while awake.

I thought it might help if I set a very specific goal for overcoming the bedwetting problem. At the beginning of the session, with Tommy on the massage table, I suggested he shoot for four dry nights between our sessions. I provided him with some techniques, which would allow him to visualize this goal. I asked, "what was the driest thing you can think of?" He said, "the desert." I then had him visualize himself standing in the desert, smiling, holding a big number four. He laughed when he visualized the image, indicating he found it emotionally valuable.

I then suggested Tommy imagine the little two-year-old boy inside himself. I spoke to the inner two-year-old as if I was speaking with a two year old about ways to connect with his mother now, about how happy it would make her if he grew up to be a self-reliant ten-year-old. As I spoke with him about meeting his own needs, Tommy's body began twisting and turning, with only Carol's hands supporting his movements. It seemed clear my suggestion that he meet his own needs triggered a release of long-held emotional energies.

At our next appointment, I greeted Tommy and his father in the waiting room. As the three of us were alone, I sat next to Tommy, slapped my thighs, took a deep breath, and as if feigning great ceremony asked, "Well, Thomas, how did you do this week?" Tommy smiled sheepishly and looked at his feet. His father's smile lit up the room. "He had three dry nights," his dad said, beaming.

With concern, Tommy's father spoke of the night before this session. His son had endured a horrific nightmare, after having been free of them earlier in the week. The nightmare, Tommy's father added, came on a night when he had wet the bed. When he said this

I was struck by the thought that perhaps Tommy's bedwetting might be related to the nightmare in a different way. What if this was the way Tommy woke himself while he was having a nightmare? The idea seemed worth pursuing.

Upon entering the therapy room, Tommy got up on the table without coaxing. He enjoyed the idea he had some dry nights and his attitude was one of a person ready to work. Carol reminded me about the energy blockage in his throat she had identified during the last session. With this in mind, I suggested that some nightmares might be so scary he couldn't wake himself up. and perhaps the two-year-old had created a way to escape from the dream by wetting the bed.

At this realization, Tommy's body began to shake, once again indicating a noticeable release of energy. Carol had me place my hand gently on his throat as she worked in the area of the sacrum. I told Tommy his throat had become clear and his voice was powerful enough to allow him to yell in his dreams, loud enough to awaken himself whenever he needed to. He moaned gently as the energy started to move from his throat. The physical release prompted by this suggestion was palpable, like little sparks of static electricity dancing beneath my fingertips.

Following this initial burst, there were several additional powerful releases from the boy's throat. I told Tommy he should be kind to his inner two-year-old, because of how hard the inner version of himself worked to protect him. I reassured him, nightmares are normal, when a two-year-olds mother was very sad and especially when she was absent. I suggested he stop being angry with the little guy, and start to appreciate and even love him for his good work.

Tommy came to the next session with his mother. He proudly looked me right in the eye and told me he had managed five dry nights during that past week. I indicated my pleasure at the improvement. However, the fact that he had not gone symptom-free led me to believe we had overlooked something. Bearing this in mind, I focused the session on the issue of identifying and eliminating whatever obstacles remained.

Tommy's mother remained in the room with us during this session. She held his hand as he went through yet another series of releases. Tommy squeezed his mother's hand tightly and began to mouth the word "Momma" repeatedly. This slipped by me initially, but Tommy's mother made a point of calling it to my attention.

Tommy appeared stunned as he sat up at the end of our session. He looked at his mother. "It's okay for you to hug her right now," I whispered gently. Tommy sprang off the table and into her arms. They hugged each other for quite some time. As I watched, I felt the child was truly resolving his early emotional wound.

It was shortly after this work that Tommy reported he managed to stay dry every night. I spoke with his father about six months later, and learned Tommy experienced only one bout of bedwetting, which occurred during a particularly stressful time. Fortunately, the episode only lasted a week, and when the stressful situation was resolved, Tommy's bed became "dry as a desert" once again.

7. SURGERY

"Winning is overrated. The only time it is really
important is in surgery and war."
–Al McGuire

Surgery can be characterized as wounding in order to heal. The physical trauma that comes from the surgeon's scalpel, as well as, any uncertainty a patient may have regarding the procedure naturally makes an surgery emotionally stressful. Ernest Rossi, PhD, and David Cheek, MD, in their book Mind-Body Therapy, state that mind-body awareness of surgical events is not an unusual phenomenon.

Carol: Aware While Under Anesthesia

My initial insight that surgical events have the potential for patient awareness and emotional consequences came from one of my own patients. Carol came for treatment of chronic pain that had lingered for seven agonizing years after a serious car accident. When I asked her to describe the wreck and subsequent surgery, she looked at me for a few seconds, as if sizing me up. "I remember awakening during surgery and being aware of the whole thing."

When Carol's surgeon came to check in on her the morning after the surgery, she related her unusual experience. He assured her the experience she described was nothing more than a dream. His gentle demeanor shifted dramatically when she repeated several things she had heard him say while under anesthesia, even detailing an account of an argument with his wife. As the color drained from his face, he hastily left the room. Carol reported the surgeon would never speak with her directly again. She had much difficulty in recovering post surgery. She felt crushed that the surgeon would not admit to what had obviously occurred, and felt she could not trust him any longer. This led to Carol's exploration of a lifelong pattern of difficulty in trusting authority figures or significant others that began when her parents did not believe she had been molested by a babysitter.

While it is powerful and instructive to work with patients at a deep level and go through the process with them, it is always more powerful to have a personal experience, as I did with my own surgical adventure. I'll share my own story with you now.

My Leg Remembers Surgery

In January 1995, I had surgery for a serious knee injury. Several weeks into my post-operative rehabilitation, I was ready to do some emotional release work of my own. At the time I was working with massage therapist, Lisa Rose. I asked her if she felt comfortable doing release work on me. She agreed to help. Once on the therapy table, I quickly descended into a deep trance state. My injured leg soon began to move strangely, achieving angles of contortion that would be very difficult, if not impossible, for me to replicate. Confused and upset by these strange and involuntary movements, I asked the therapist for an explanation regarding what was occurring.

"I think your leg is remembering the surgery," she explained. "Next time you see your surgeon, show him what your leg did during our session."

About two weeks later I described the odd event to the surgeon. He started to laugh. "Tell your therapist I had a lot of trouble lining your leg up correctly during the surgery. I had to call in a second surgeon to assist. The positions you described were the precise angles we used to align your leg during the surgery. "it wasn't easy," he replied. Then he added, "As you were leaving the surgical theatre, I whispered in your ear, "You're going to get all better." I guess it worked because the surgery was a success.

Helen's Surgeon Was Impaired

Helen, a very accomplished thirty-nine-year-old college administrator, suffered from chronic anxiety. She believed her anxiety originated about a year prior to our meeting, following a series of negative interactions with her physicians. She requested that I use the Emotional Shifting Process to treat her.

The Information Detector (I.D.) indicated the point of origin of Helen's anxiety was age twenty-five. Speaking in pressured tones, she began to discuss a surgery she had undergone at that time.

Helen recalled she had been fearful she would die during the procedure. Indeed, she had even dreamt about her forthcoming surgery in a prophetic manner, perhaps anticipating her terror. She told me that on the morning of the procedure, she had been heavily sedated, so as not to be a bother to the nurses. As she discussed the behavior and motives of these health-care professionals, Helen began to seethe with anger.

I requested that she try to observe the scene more directly. She indicated she could see the surgical theatre clearly in her mind's eye. Suddenly she cried out, "The surgeon is drunk! He made a crooked incision, and cut my kidney instead of my gall bladder."

Apparently, a nurse interceded, preventing the physician from inflicting further damage. Helen began to experience sharp and unrelenting pain. She felt as if she were dying and became very angry with the surgeon.

Excitedly, Helen said, "I'm leaving my body and traveling down a long tube, to a light. I hear a voice telling me to go back, that I'm needed to raise my sons."

After coming out of trance, Helen exclaimed, "I knew I had died on that operating table! They didn't tell me because they were protecting the doctor."

A few months later, when Helen returned home to Indiana for a vacation, she attempted to research the medical records of her surgery. She was unable find them, however, her eighty-four-year-old aunt knew what had become of the doctor who had injured her. Helen was stunned when her aunt told her the physician had his license to practice medicine revoked for operating while intoxicated. She was angry that a drunk surgeon had operated on her, but felt vindicated to realize her inner compass had been on target.

Howard's Journey To The Other Side

Howard, a 42 year old businessman, experienced both chronic pain and depression for over two years. He recalled the incident as if it were a video replayed in slow motion: While in his automobile, waiting for a red light to change, he glanced in his rearview mirror. To his horror, he saw a car careening toward him out of control. In the auto directly in front of him, several older people also waited for the traffic light to change.

"I quickly arched my back and pressed my right foot as hard as I could on the brake, so I would bear the brunt of the impact myself and avoid striking the car in front of me." He continued, "Thank God I managed to miss the other car, sparing the old people any harm."

About twenty-four hours after the impact, Howard began to experience pain from the middle of his back to his shoulders. The chronic ache forced Howard to see a neurosurgeon. After suffering through a battery of diagnostic procedures, he was informed by his physician he would need surgery to correct serious problems with the discs in his spinal cord. According to the surgeon, the procedure went well, nonetheless, Howard's discomfort worsened. He felt hopeless and depressed. Due to the physical manifestation of his condition, I asked Howard to consider the Emotional Shifting Process.

Carol Martin assisted me with Howard. Once he

was on the therapeutic table, Howard described his pain as "a steel licorice stick" that went from his mid-back all the way through his left shoulder. The I.D. indicated his surgery was an important component to understanding his pain. As he was waiting in the surgical prep room for the procedure to commence, he had the realization that he might die. He became very frightened, and began to cry. A nurse, noticing his emotional discomfort, gave him a tranquilizer. A few minutes later, he fell asleep.

Once the operation began, he felt himself lift out of his body and float to "the other side," where he saw many family members who had passed on. He felt a tremendous sense of peace. He contemplated the possibility of allowing himself to die and remaining there, but decided to return. At the end of our session, he got off the therapeutic table with tears in his eyes, embracing Carol and me.

By the next session, Howard's depression had lifted so dramatically that his coworkers expressed curiosity about what had contributed to such a marked improvement in his mood. However, the pain in his neck remained.

During our next Emotional Shifting Process, Howard experienced a previously forgotten time. When he was four years old, Howard remembered a vacation to the California shore with his parents, He recalled many of the minute details of that day, such as the bright red sweater he had been wearing. He described joyfully jumping into the ocean, whose deep blue color fascinated him. When he hit the chilly water, Howard stared in wonder at the soft blue "blanket" of water around him. The next thing he knew, his father had frantically pulled him up and out of the water by the neckline of his sweater. Although this action had wrenched his neck, Howard said he was more upset about being jolted from his reverie than by any physical discomfort. Such was not the case for his hysterical parents, who screamed at him and then at each other. They had lost a child before he was born. He had the sense this incident triggered a terrible memory for them. Upon returning to their rental cabin, his parents dried him off and wrapped him snugly in blankets. He felt good nestling in the warm quilts, but was bothered by their continued arguing, "That's when my neck began to hurt," he said.

When Howard reported for our next session, he appeared significantly more energetic. He moved more quickly than before, conversed with crispness and self-assurance, and smiled more frequently. He had given up his usual subdued and somber tones in favor of brighter, happier colors. "I was not depressed last week," he reported. "And my pain has diminished significantly."

Together we scrutinized an overview of his past traumas. He revisited the scene of being alone in the hospital prior to his surgery and the episode that had occurred at the ocean. For the first time, Howard began to separate the transcendent experiences he enjoyed while under anesthesia and submerged in seawater from the fear he had felt during his surgery and his parents' quarrel at the ocean.

For several additional sessions we worked to integrate these insights into Howard's daily life.

During this time, Howard became increasingly aware that when he meditated or allowed himself to become absorbed listening to music, his pain dissipated almost entirely. Conversely, when he neglected his need for deep relaxation, his pain returned. We came to the understanding that his depression related to his prior inability to meet his own inner needs. Pleased with his progress, feeling he gained insight into his problems and now had workable strategies for coping with his symptoms, Howard concluded therapy.

Edith's Post Surgical Pain

Another patient whose symptoms connected to a surgical procedure was Edith, a retired schoolteacher. Before being diagnosed with cancer, she had been a vigorous and energetic sixty-two-year-old who enjoyed spending her newfound leisure time traveling, gardening, and painting. Six months before our meeting, she had undergone surgery to remove a tumor in her chest. According to her surgeon, the operation had been uneventful and successful, but she awakened from the anesthetic to excruciating pain, a condition that continued to plague her since that day. The pain dramatically restricted Edith's life. She became increasingly depressed and withdrawn. By the time I met her, Edith was experiencing suicidal thoughts.

Edith was very sensitive to the implication that her pain could be psychological in origin. She regarded any suggestion of an emotional or psychological component to her discomfort as a validation of her surgeon's assertions that her pain was really "in her head." It was clear to me she only would feel comfortable giving me permission to work with her if the body was the focus of our consideration. Physical Therapist, Grace Walters, worked with me on this patient.

Our initial sessions with Edith helped me to understand the depth of her unexpressed rage. Life had rarely met her expectations, and she often felt like people were violating her boundaries. However, she found anger very difficult to express. During the succeeding weeks of therapy, she related her experiences with considerably more emotion. She then revealed her overwhelming fear concerning cancer.

Edith described the way she learned of her cancer diagnosis: She had gone to her physician for a routine physical examination prior to a vacation cruise. Her doctor's report indicated she had a malignancy. This was a crushing blow, and she instantly envisioned a lonely and horrible existence, followed by a painful death. In the next session, Edith spoke with raw emotion as she pictured herself lying on a gurney outside the operating room, alone and frightened. She recalled feeling overwhelmed as tears silently streamed down her face while she anticipated the surgeon's scalpel.

As we continued our sessions, and Edith grew more comfortable, she was able to reach more deeply into herself. She visualized events that transpired while she was in surgery. She "saw" that her ribs had been spread too far apart, and suspected she had been unnecessarily injured. Edith described intense anger toward her surgeon. Each time the surgeon told her he couldn't understand why she had so much pain, her inner turmoil increased. On the therapeutic table, she was finally able to verbalize the full extent of her rage.

Once she allowed herself this emotional release, Edith began to heal. Her symptoms of depression receded and her pain diminished. In the following session, Edith reconstructed her terrifying fear when she had contemplated suffering and dying by herself. Facing her feelings, she wept as if she were a child, while Grace held her.

In the months that followed she participated in a pain management protocol. She reported enjoying longer pain-free periods during her day. The difference in her outlook astonished and delighted her. She engaged energetically in an exercise regimen that strengthened her body and increasde her flexibility. She gained the focus to track and understand how to move her body in a healthy manner, along with time-management skills. These tools gave her the ability to effectively manage her pain. She was pleased with her progress and optimistic about the future. Having accomplished these objectives, she resumed her everyday activities and put down a deposit for her long-delayed vacation.

8. TRAUMA

What caused us each to live hidden?
A wound, the wind, a word, a parent.
Sometimes we wait in a helpless way,
Awkwardly, not whole and not healed.
When we hid the wound, we fell back
From a human to a shelled life.
Now we feel the ant's hard chest,
The carapace, the silent tongue.
This must be the way of the ant,
The winter ant, the way of those
Who are wounded and want to live,
To breathe, to sense another, and to wait.
–Robert Bly

Trauma, the primary metaphor of our times, is possibly the greatest challenge to modern psychotherapy. The word trauma comes from the Greek, "to wound." The Merriam-Webster Dictionary defines trauma as "a disordered psychic or behavioral state resulting from severe mental or emotional stress or physical injury."

Our understanding of the psychological aftermath of trauma has been advanced by observations of the postwar problems exhibited by combat veterans of recent wars, in addition to the profound effects of childhood sexual abuse. The constellation of emotional symptoms associated with exposure to traumatic events has been accorded a separate designation in the Diagnostic and Statistical Manual for Psychiatry (DSM-V). The category in which they appear is called Post Traumatic Stress Disorder (PTSD).

In my experience, the hallmark of trauma is an internal reaction to a devastating situation so overwhelming to a person that his or her ability to cope is compromised. Stress reactions are psychological and often physiological in nature. They also may result in severe anxiety, depression, rage, terror, anguish, horror, flashbacks, nightmares, and a sense that one will not have a full life or satisfying relationships. Trauma may or may not involve bodily injury, it may be a singular or repeat event, and the source may be natural or man made. There may be the experience of betrayal, loss of control, and a complete lack of safety. As there is often a bodily component to trauma, and a psycho-physiological component, treatment of trauma is well served by the Emotional Shifting Process, as the body is considered at the same time we address the mental/emotional state.

My personal entrée into the world of trauma came when I was an intern at the Palo Alto VA Medical Center in Palo Alto, California. As a young intern, I encountered a patient there who was, for me, an example of a nightmare case. Norman was morbidly obese, had COPD, was addicted to pain medication, and experienced panic attacks. When I inquired if he had seen combat, he immediately began to unravel. Although I was not an experienced therapist at the time, I knew enough to attempt to get him to slow down. He would not or could not gain control of himself, and subsequent sessions generated more anxiety and anguish. Norman's case was made more interesting for me by the fact that I was being supervised by a man I respected deeply, the Chief of Psychological Services for the entire hospital, Dr. Eugene Zukowsky.

The day after the fourth session, I found Norman in the hallway of the clinic shouting in the loudest voice possible that "Richard Schulman" had ruined his life. Unable to calm him down, I walked to the next building to inform my supervisor of the situation, thinking he should hear this from me rather than those who were experiencing the ruckus in the clinic. I was discovering in real time that conventional psychotherapy had limitations when dealing with trauma, as the energy of the trauma surfaced, but did not have an exit point, leaving Norman and patients like him feeling worse rather than better.

Dr. Zukowsky was more than kind to me. He informed me I had met my "humbler," and if I ever thought I was really good at my job, that I should remember this day and remain humble. He then went on to relate his own experience with a patient who taught him the same lesson. He advised me that although my confidence had been shaken (it had), I was going to be okay and that I would be good at my profession. Sadly, he told me he had lost confidence in the field of psychology. That hit me hard. I determined in that moment that I would never have a conversation like this with a student or anyone else and would find a way to help others deal with such horrible pain. While that was the last time I saw Norman, the impact of the day was not lost on me. I had to find something that worked better. The catalyst that led to the creation of the Emotional Shifting Process began to bubble inside of me.

Everyone has different event triggers they find personally upsetting. The decisions a trauma survivor makes may be based on family of origin experiences, and/or on biological factors, such as genetics or temperament. Individuals who have experienced traumatic events as children are more likely to be adversely affected by trauma later in life. The diverse spectrum of responses is evident during natural disasters, such as earthquakes and hurricanes, or man-made calamities like plane crashes, where large numbers of people, exposed to the same circumstances, have widely varying psychological reactions after the event.

When trauma occurs during childhood, a patient's report of the incident is most likely to be relayed to the therapist through the perception, cognition, and emotions of a child. In instances of child abuse, for example, the issue of the relationship between the victim and perpetrator assumes greater importance, as bonds regarding love, trust, and protection in many case have been violated. It appears betrayal by someone whom the trauma survivor depended upon for physical or emotional survival produces serious psychological consequences, akin to those resulting from life-threatening traumas.

James, The Tennis Pro

Perhaps due to its weather, the Gulf Coast of Florida is home to a large number of professional athletes. As a lifelong sports enthusiast, I feel privileged when I have the opportunity to work with one of these athletes. James, a well-known professional tennis player had ended the previous playing season on a sour note, having incurred an injury to his abdomen, which remained unhealed. His strength was sapped, his confidence diminished, and his once-great love for the game was slipping.

When his condition persisted, the advice to James from his trainer was to "just gut it out." With his injury having failed to heal over the winter, and a new season just around the corner, his anxiety was understandably high. James told me the sports psychologist he consulted was in agreement with the trainers and doctors. In their opinion, he was malingering and they strongly suggested he put more energy into his training. By the time James contacted me, he was entertaining the idea that perhaps the problem was in his head. He asked me to "hypnotize it away."

James proved to be an extraordinary hypnotic subject. His powers of inner focus and concentration were superb, as he was eager and cooperative. However, even with his impressive work, the symptoms did not improve. When I suggested the Emotional Shifting Process, he showed enthusiasm, perhaps more out of desperation than faith.

I engaged Carol Martin to work with me. As the first session unfolded, James began to speak about a situation that had occurred during the off-season, following his first year in college. He had been working in the construction trade, and felt the supervisor on the job detested him. His boss was unrelenting in the criticism directed towards James. When James suffered an injury while lifting some heavy boards, the supervisor launched into an angry tirade, humiliating James in front of the rest of the crew. As James began to recall the angry feelings associated with this incident, his body responded to the memory with a gentle, but persistent vibration in his abdomen, revealing a release of emotional energy.

During the following session, James was able to access even deeper levels within himself. He relayed an experience that occurred while playing Little League baseball. His older brother, a shortstop, was playing for the opposing team. James hit a solid line drive. As he was rounding second base and heading for third, his brother slyly stuck out his leg and tripped him. He fell, and felt something "grab" in his stomach. As he lay sprawled on the ground in obvious pain, his brother came over and tagged him out. Apparently not content with merely impeding and hurting James, his brother seemed determined to degrade him. He further humiliated James as he lay on the field by screaming insults at him.

When this hidden pain began to unfold, James thrashed about and liberated imprisoned emotional energy from his body. Carol provided support to his body as he writhed, while I encouraged James to continue to talk about his emotions. He wept as he remembered all the times his brother had mistreated him. When engaging these events emotionally, James cried out again and again in his pain. At the end of the session he was extremely fatigued, but felt a peace he had not known in years.

After several Emotional Shifting Process sessions, James engaged in some traditional, conversational therapy. The purpose was to provide support that would enable him to make sense of the material he accessed in the Emotional Shifting Process. For the first time in his life, James was able to understand his tendency to be passive in many areas of life. Despite his amazing physical gifts, his mental outlook constricted his competetive fire and impeded progress in his sport.

When these sessions were completed, James was feeling consistently confident with respect to the new tennis season and optimistic about a full physical recovery. Some months later, he reported the injury had healed beautifully. He went on to have one of the finest seasons of his professional tennis career.

Vera: Scared To Death

Vera was another patient who had a profound experience while working with the Emotional Shifting Process. One of the first things I noticed about Vera was what appeared to be a permanent frozen smile on her face. In fact, she grinned even while telling me how angry and unhappy she was. I asked why she beamed while speaking about such uncomfortable material. She replied that she realized she smiled all the time, but was as perplexed by her behavior as I was.

Vera re-experienced her painful reactions to her mother's controlling, vicious, and demeaning manner during the Emotional Shifting Process. Her recollections seemed to explain her fear and depression, yet she remained unable to understand her permanent smile even when she felt miserable.

The breakthrough session started out rather routinely. I requested that Vera return to the age and circumstances in which her permanent smile had originated. The I.D. indicated the origin of her symptoms was located at age ten. Vera spontaneously described, in detail, the living room of her childhood home. As she did, tears started to form in her eyes.

"I'm on the couch reading," she recalled, "sitting precariously on the edge; you know how kids do. My mother came into the room unexpectedly, and yelled so loudly that I fell off the couch and fainted. The next thing I remembered is waking up in the bathroom with her splashing water in my face."

"Vera," I suggested, "look carefully at what happens to you when you begin to hear her, right before you black out. Please, go very slowly." Vera slowed down perceptibly as she began to relate the story again. Second by second she brought herself toward, into, and through the process. As she did, she surprised even herself as she felt herself leave her body in response to the unexpectedness and power of her mother's furious and caustic yell.

"Where are you?" I inquired. Vera was silent, but visibly anxious. "I don't know," she responded. "Everything is a black cloud." The level of anxiety apparent in her face and in her physical posture increased markedly. Her body started to shake. "I think I'm dead," she sobbed. "Get a fan or something," I advised Vera, "and blow that black cloud away, so you can see."

Moments later, having calmed considerably, Vera continued. "I can see the living room," she told me. "My mom is standing over me, trying to wake me up. I'm kind of glad, because I think she's feeling guilty." Vera started to laugh ever so slightly. "She's taking me over to the bathroom," she explained, "and I'm waking up now." In a flash of insight, Vera exclaimed, "I think that I smile all the time so she won't yell at me and kill me."

I again asked Vera to go back to the onset of the verbal assault, but to remain at the point at which she began to leave her body. Once she was able to comply, I suggested, "See if you can go to a nicer place than the living room."

"How?" she inquired, quite understandably.

"Try to move through the ceiling," I proposed. "You are in the world of imagination. You can do whatever you wish." With this encouragement, Vera easily moved through the ceiling and reported she could see the rooftops of the houses below her. "Is there a nice place nearby?" I asked.

"There is a nice river behind my house," she observed. Floating toward this river, she began to speak of the peacefulness and tranquility of the scene below. She saw deer playing in the woods by the water and birds drinking at the water's edge. She expressed how very connected she felt with nature.

Her face appeared to transmute before my eyes. The false, frozen smile I was accustomed to seeing began to melt and gently eased into a more relaxed, genuine, and peaceful expression. She ended the session by drifting back to her body and remembering her wonderful inner vision, rather than her fear of death.

In the months following Vera's realization that she had smiled to prevent her mother from "killing" her, she reported she had become more authentic in her relationships with both her mother and husband, even at times when it was painful for her to do so. She continued to experience conflict with them periodically, but she no longer smiled when she was upset.

Jennifer: Molested As A Child

Jennifer, a thirty-one-year-old teacher, entered therapy with the intention of learning how to better cope with the emotional pain of her divorce. She related how she also felt extremely anxious about an anticipated visit by her parents. As the date of her parents' visit approached, her discomfort escalated markedly. Jennifer told me she had little reason to be so upset with her parents and agreed with my observation that her symptoms seemed too intense for the situation. She consented to try the Emotional Shifting Process.

Carol Martin assisted me with Jennifer's treatment. Age seven was identified as the origin of her anxiety. Jennifer described how nervous she always became when her parents went out. I requested she describe a typical scene in considerable detail. Jennifer spontaneously revealed that on one occasion, when her parents had been out, some older boys visited. With this statement, Jennifer's body began to shake. She crossed her legs when they began to tremble.

"They lured me into my parent's bedroom and stuck a flashlight inside of me," she murmured. As she began to recall the scene more vividly, Jennifer started to experience considerable pain in her genital region and lower back. As she lay on the therapy table, she wanted to scream for help. She attempted to do so, but to no avail. The scream stuck in her throat.

I whispered to her, "I'm going to count to three and then Carol will gently touch you on the throat. When you feel the touch, you can let go of the sound stuck in there." When Carol touched her she screamed and then cried dramatically, while her body shook uncontrollably. She began to talk about her unspoken shame over the incident along with a sense she was to blame. As she tearfully spoke of her long unmet need to talk to someone about what had transpired that day, her pain eased.

At the end of the session, Jennifer's face seemed to radiate light. She voiced her belief that without the body component of the treatment, it would have been very difficult for her to uncover the root cause of her distress. Jennifer later reported her visit with her parents went well. She had only encountered the normal, but predictable conflicts that occur when a child who has become an adult spends time in the company of parents who are still a bit uncomfortable with her having grown up.

A group of patients who have dire need of the Emotional Shifting Process, and great potential for healing, are veterans of military combat. It has been my privilege to work with several brave soldiers, who sacrificed themselves in the cauldron of battle. They had all spent years, sometimes decades, carrying the emotional and physical pain deep inside.

Harry, One Proud Marine
Can't Be Killed By Bullets

Harry, a highly decorated and proud US Marine, had served four tours in Vietnam and had multiple physical and emotional wounds. His appearance resembled the combination of an eagle and a bear. His arms were longer than normal for his stature as they hung by his side. He had crystalline blue eyes and an intensity of gaze that was unnerving for people who didn't know him. Apparently his code name in Vietnam was "Stoneman." He came to me expressing a desire to work on depression, anxiety, and chronic pain symptoms. Harry was working as a security expert and personal bodyguard. He felt his work was beginning to suffer due to his symptoms. He said, "I don't want to turn into a cartoon; the Vietnam vet who is depressed, drinking, and can't hold a job."

Harry related three main traumas that troubled him deeply. The first was being caught in a bear trap, a type of booby trap, while on patrol in the jungle. The bear trap was a large hole, covered by leaves. holding a smaller hole with spikes that closed upon the soldier's foot. He spoke about the unrelenting apprehension the troops experienced regarding booby traps. During our initial interview, he described the incident without much emotion. Since his lower right leg held much of his pain, I suspected he would need to process this experience. With the help of physical therapist, Grace Walters, we ventured into what became dangerous territory for Harry, and us, as well.

Harry was an excellent hypnotic subject. I used a visualization to help him relax and access his inner world. Grace began to tune into his body, while in his mind Harry responded to my suggestion that he travel to the time at which his leg pain originated. Grace signaled me the I.D. indicated Harry was accessing emotionally important material.

Harry began showing signs of going into a very deep trance state. His breathing slowed and his eyes began to move as though in a waking dream. I asked him where he was and he whispered, "I'm on patrol. Charlie (Viet Cong) has booby trapped the area. I have to be careful." He began to sweat profusely, He then reacted as if hit by something as Grace was working on his lower leg. Harry showed extreme tension in his body and did not respond to my voice.

Harry was stuck in the bear trap. At first he went limp, but slowly, his large right hand began to ball into a fist. Grace, who was touching his leg to help create an exit for the emotional energy to release, was in the range of it and in danger of being hit. I had the alarming notion Harry was experiencing a flashback. I sensed he "saw" Grace as a Viet Cong soldier who discovered him in the trap. Deciding to put myself in harms way, I quickly moved next to his ear and whispered, "Harry, this is Rich. You are remembering something terrible, but it's a memory from the past, not from now. I would never let anything bad happen to you. Please don't hurt Grace, she is here to help you." As I spoke, his hand began to relax and we were able to complete our session without incident.

Harry related later that while in the bear trap, a Viet Cong soldier approached and taunted him, thinking the American soldier was dead. When he came close, Harry knocked him out with a punch from his right hand. He was then able to get to his knife and kill his enemy. He managed to extricate himself from the bear trap, but not without significant damage to his leg. Following the session, Harry reported that the pain in his leg was much relieved.

Opening this material brought some pain relief, but emotionally he was less stable than before. Harry's massive defense structure had been breached and long held emotion was leaking out. Harry recognized he was in trouble and agreed to come in again. When he returned, he was able to consciously access two different traumas connected by feelings of guilt. The first was his guilt of surviving the war when some of his buddies did not, the second, involved the inadvertent killing of an innocent man.

Harry was proud of his American Indian ancestry. He likened himself to Geronimo, the Indian who could not be shot by bullets. I once asked him how he got his Bronze Star. He told me about a firefight in which several of his men had been killed by the enemy in a machine gun nest. He related that he walked right up to the nest, dropped a hand grenade into it, killing the operator and silencing the guns.

After relating that story, he said, "You know, when my buddies died, I went crazy, but in a non-emotional kind of way. It wasn't bravery, because I wasn't scared.

I didn't care if I lived or died. I don't know how they didn't kill me. I just decided to walk over there and knock them down (kill them)." Then he revealed the emotional stuck place. "I was their leader," he intoned. "I should have died with them." He wept with guilt that he had survived and two of his guys had not.

Grace placed her hand on his heart, and I asked, "Did any of the other guys survive because you took out the machine gun?" He nodded. "Please put that into your emotional equation," I said. Survivor's guilt is part of the deal when you are a Marine.

Harry nodded again, and then said, "Marine's don't leave anyone behind. We'd risk our lives to bring out the body of one of our guys."

"Did you bring those guys home?" I asked. He nodded 'yes,' again. "Go into the other world," I encouraged him. "Find the men you lost and ask them if they blame you."

He began to smile. "I haven't seen my friends in a long time. They are giving me a hard time for being so hard on myself. Gallagher just said, 'Stop being an old woman. Get over it. We are okay.'"

The last incident was perhaps the most difficult for the Marine. Harry related that he was on a mission to take out a man who specialized in killing American troops from afar. In other words, a sniper. "We supposedly had good intel," he told us. "There he was, right where he was supposed to be, in that fishing village, in his black pajamas and large black hat, doing exactly what they told me he would be doing," he said. Harry picked up an imaginary rifle, as if reliving the scene in his mind. "I was a thousand yards away, but it was a makeable shot," he continued. Then he pulled an imaginary trigger. "I watched as he slumped after being shot and his hat came off." Harry stopped. One tear came out of his left eye. "It was an old man. I killed an old fisherman."

Harry became enraged as he related this to his entire war experience. "I was a patriot," he exclaimed. "I wanted to serve our country, but those bastards didn't care what happened. It was never about protecting our country. I wasn't there to kill innocent old men. They lied to me repeatedly. A lot of good men died. This is on my ticket forever." Grace held him gently as he cried.

Harry was on a journey back to his own heart. He was able to let go of much of the trauma from the war and became more loving towards his friends and family. He was better than ever at his job, because, as he told me, "I can be relaxed and dynamic at the same time."

The expectation that a psychotherapist must be capable of addressing the most traumatic events in a patient's life is not a recent one. Addressing the body component of trauma during the Emotional Shifting Process offers hope for patients who have not received relief from conventional psychotherapeutic approaches. The psychotherapist's responsibility is to meet a patient where his or her truth exists, to help them attain greater freedom of emotional expression, and a more satisfying relationship with themselves, their significant others, and the world in which they live.

9. DEATH: COMMUNICATION WITH THE OTHER SIDE

"While I thought that I was learning how to live,
I have been learning how to die."
–Leonardo da Vinci

Loss, death, and grief are often to be key issues in psychotherapy. As the noted spiritual teacher, Ram Dass, explained, the decision to engage in any relationship is a decision to experience grief. All relationships begin and end in separation. The truth behind this assertion is no more apparent than when we consider how unlikely it is for partners in the most loving, long-term relationship to die at the same time. One will die first. Both will experience loss.

Although conventional psychotherapy addresses the formidable emotions surrounding death, it is not always comfortable dealing with the uncommon repercussions they can create. Author and grief counselor, Louis LaGrand, Ph.D, reviewed many studies of after-death communication and concluded that in this realm, "the extraordinary is ordinary." He found that the experience of a living person encountering a loved one who has just died is a reasonably commonplace event. He believed, however, that many of these individuals suppress open expression of these incidents for fear of being ridiculed. In my experience, exploring such after-death communication and the accompanying emotions associated with the phenomena has a profoundly healing effect on patients.

The number of people reporting communication with a deceased loved one is astonishing. Sociologist and Roman Catholic priest, Father Andrew Greeley, then at the University of Chicago National Opinion Research Council, interviewed more than a thousand people to learn whether they believed they had ever experienced genuine contact with a deceased person. Almost half reported they had. Moreover, two-thirds of the women in this study said they communicated with their departed husbands.

W. Dewi Rees, writing in the British Medical Journal, reported approximately fifty percent of the 282 widows and widowers he interviewed had transpersonal contact with, or hallucinations of, their deceased spouses. Physician Richard Olsen and his colleagues discovered that sixty-one percent of widows in their study claimed to be in touch with their departed husbands. In all of these studies, the majority of the surviving partners felt the experience played a "positive to profound" role in their emotional healing.

David's Mother Says Goodbye

David, a thirty-two-year-old, single, self-employed businessman, sought psychotherapy at the insistence of his girlfriend. She felt that David would begin to withdraw emotionally whenever they began to grow close. David acknowledged the intimacy issues and said, he said he was willing to work on them. Massage Therapist, Carol Martin, worked with me.

In our first session, the I.D. indicated age nine was an important time in the patient's life with regard to intimacy. We later learned this was the age when David first realized his mother was ill and might die. In addition, it was a time when the family's overriding concerns about his mother's malady left him in need of emotional support and reassurance. As David began to re-experience the early circumstances during our initial session, he began to see how his fear of his mother's dying caused him to distance himself from close relationships and create walls to keep him from feeling deep emotions.

At the beginning of our second session, age five was targeted as a emotionally charged period to explore. David said even at that young age, he realized his emotional needs were not going to be met by his mother, as she had turned to alcohol in an attempt to cope with her rapidly declining health. Upon entering a trance state, David began to absorb this concept on an emotional level. He spontaneously recalled the night his mother had died when he was nine years old. I suggested he examine this material slowly and carefully.

"She was at home, and the family was sitting on the couch watching TV," he related. "I got tired and went to bed. My dad woke me up later and told me that she had died." David seemed oddly devoid of the emotion one would normally expect to accompany the expression of such a traumatic event, so I recommended he reexamine the occurrence.

This he did, painstakingly, and in minute detail, reconstructing each event, from his time on the couch, to the moment he drifted off to sleep. Throughout his retelling, David's emotions remained flat. He lacked the animated quality usually found in nine-year old boys. I perceived this as a reflection of what he had to do to survive then, where he was stuck now in his difficulty engaging his emotions.

I suggested he repeat the process again, even more slowly. He agreed to try. Once he reached the point where he got into bed, I leaned over and whispered, "David, go to sleep now and tell me your dreams." With that, as if my words had granted a sort of "psychological permission" to unleash his bound feelings, he exploded with emotion, sobbing loudly, and his words began to tumble out of him with great pressure.

"She came to me to say goodbye." As he spoke, David's body tensed and relaxed several times as he also experienced a physical release of energy. Carol later told me that his sacrum had begun to vibrate and release emotional energy immediately prior to his emotional breakthrough.

Although he had a memory of his dream, David pushed it out of his ordinary awareness and had never before spoken to anyone about this profound life experience. After our sessions, he gradually began to gain a new sense of himself, an awareness that was more complete, and that allowed him to become more peaceful. He was also able to experience true intimacy with his girlfriend, whom he later married.

Olive's Death Anxiety

The next example of after-death communication was that of Olive. Olive, a thirty two year old mother of two young children, had suffered from severe anxiety periodically throughout her adult life. Having recently obtained employment as a nurse in a cardiac unit, she subsequently began experiencing a series of decidedly unpleasant interactions with staff members in her new work environment. She appeared to have responded to these incidents with a series of debilitating anxiety attacks, several of which verged on overwhelming her.

Assisted by Massage Therapist, Carol Martin, and using I.D. as a guide, we ascertained age five as a reasonable starting point to explore the origins of Olive's anxiety. The patient described her childhood home and her family of origin in considerable detail. She lived in the back room of the house. As she spoke her voice began to decrease in volume until it was almost a whisper. She descended further and further into trance, and I asked her what it was like for her to be in that room again. She answered that it was lonely, and then almost in response to hearing her own words, she began to feel intense sadness and fear.

She recalled during her early childhood that her grandmother had shared the room with her. She remembered her parents sent her away just before her grandmother's death. Never having had the opportunity to say good-bye to her grandmother, whom she dearly loved, affected her profoundly. She acknowledged, "I knew grandma was dead, but I couldn't admit it to myself." With these words, her voice began to sound like that of a little girl. "I knew grandma was gone because she came to me to say good-bye," she said, her eyes moist with tears.

Following these emotionally insightful experiences, Olive enjoyed several days of relief from her symptoms. This respite, however, proved to be of short duration. She called reporting a relapse. Her breathing difficulties had recurred, and her physician could find no physical explanation.

During our next session, the I.D. indicated 21 as an appropriate age for exploration. Upon hearing this, Olive instantly responded that this was the age when she had been involved in an automobile accident, where a female pedestrian had been killed.

Initially, as she uncovered and communicated information, the patient remained calm and relaxed. Shortly thereafter, however, she reported, "My legs are getting tingly." Then she began to exhibit overt indications of a significant increase in anxiety. "I'm very cold," she gasped, "It's hard to breathe." Olive then began to move about on the therapeutic table until she was lying face down. The expression reflected in her eyes and mouth was one of stark terror. "I can feel her dying," she screamed, referring to the woman who had been killed. Olive began to tremble and quiver. I had the distinct impression the body position she had assumed was not her own, but was mirroring the death throes of the expiring woman. I suggested to her that she release the woman's energy and let her go.

Olive had been certain she had resolved her feelings regarding this incident many years before. However she also recalled relating to her husband she had experienced the sensation her heart had been broken at the time of the woman's death.

She began to recall additional details about the event. She remembered the woman had been dressed completely in black. Owing to the hour of the evening, she was not readily visible. Olive related that a passerby had spoken to her after the accident. Apparently, the woman did not even look up at the oncoming traffic as she began to cross the street. Olive's breathing eased. She was finally able to relax deeply. During the following weeks, she reported that the improvement regarding her anxiety symptoms continued to appear intact.

The last story has meaning for me over and above the goodness of helping others navigate difficult waters. It involved a relationship with a person I knew as a colleague in life who had passed on.

Edgar and Connie: Healing From The Other Side

A local psychiatrist named Edgar referred a patient to me for regression therapy. He telephoned shortly afterward to discuss the patient and her problem. Edgar's phone voice was pleasing, very friendly, almost soothing. I decided I would like to meet him, so I invited him to lunch. Two weeks later, we met, enjoyed a pleasant meal and an uplifting conversation. We shared many common interests, including a love of music and sports, and an appreciation for the power of the psychotherapeutic relationship. There was, though, one area we agreed to disagree on: past-life regression therapy and reincarnation. I found these topics of great interest. Edgar, to put it mildly, did not.

Fortunately, the patient progressed in her healing, and she reported her satisfaction to Edgar. While this did not alter his views regarding reincarnation, he felt my work was effective and began to refer some of his more difficult patients for consultation. Edgar later told me he saw me as his "ninth-inning relief pitcher;" someone who could come in with the bases loaded, one out, and help him resolve a difficult situation.

For a while, Edgar and I met for lunch every few months, but eventually we began to drift apart. I had become very busy in my practice and assumed that he, too, was engrossed in his work. About a year after my last lunch with Edgar, I received a telephone call from a woman named Connie, who asked for an appointment. She said she would like to work on the area of grieving. As Connie had kept her maiden name, I had no way of knowing at the time she was Edgar's wife.

At our first session, Connie was very friendly, She acted as if she already knew me. She was candid and emotional as she discussed how her life had disintegrated since the death of her husband due to a heart attack, three months earlier. As we delved into her marriage history, it became increasingly apparent to me that the man with whom she had shared so much of her life was Edgar. The unfolding realization left me feeling increasingly uncomfortable. Finally, I asked, "Are you Edgar's wife?"

A pained yet puzzled expression fixed across her face. I was stunned. "Edgar is dead?" "Yes," she answered. "Didn't you know?" "Oh my God," I replied. "I'm so sorry. No, I didn't."

Connie had done her best to mask her grief, but she had been extremely depressed since Edgar's death. Her growing obsession with her late husband left her paralyzed when it came to attending to the practical matters of life. More often than not, Edgar had attended to those details when he was alive.

During subsequent sessions, Connie worked diligently to regain her confidence and ability to take care of herself. Her first major challenge came when she traveled to their hometown for a memorial service for Edgar's family. Connie had written a eulogy to present at the upcoming service. On the eve of departure she found herself extremely anxious.

The service was pleasant, but unremarkable. When she returned from the trip, she felt unusually and unaccountably calm. In our next session, she recalled, "I was so worried about writing that speech, I was trembling. Yet, after I calmed myself down, I found words coming to me that didn't seem like mine. They seemed like Edgar's. It was as if he had been talking to me and through me."

Connie allowed that her mood had improved following her eloquent performance at the memorial service. She did acknowledge that her low energy state and obsessive thinking had remained unaffected. After six conventional psychotherapy sessions, during which we explored her feelings about Edgar's death, Connie said she would like to see if hypnotherapy might help reach a deeper understanding of what she was experiencing. I agreed the approach might be beneficial. She was a good hypnotic subject and quickly evidenced considerable skill at entering a deep trance. From trance, she used ideo-motor signaling (responding affirmatively or negatively to my questions by raising a finger) to communicate.

At one point during a session, Connie indicated she had made a connection with Edgar. She said she felt he was sending her a message, but she couldn't understand it. I sensed it was her conscious mind keeping her from comprehending the message, so I asked to speak directly to the part of her holding the information about Edgar.

"Is Edgar there" I asked. Her Yes finger twitched and floated upwards. "Is it okay with Connie if we let his message be understood?" "Yes," the signal occurred again.

She sobbed. I encouraged her to place her hand over her heart to separate the pain she felt, while retaining the love she and her husband had shared. Connie said she could see Edgar right before her eyes. He was smiling at her, while he tenderly raised her chin and softly stroked her face. At that moment, in her mind, she knew his feelings. "He wishes I wasn't in so much pain. He is fine where he is," she said through her tears.

This session was quite a breakthrough. Connie reported great improvement in her mood and out-look. She began to take charge of her life, and shortly thereafter indicated her desire to terminate therapy. Some months later, as the one-year anniversary of Edgar's death approached, Connie grew depressed once again and contacted me. She told me she enter-tained fleeting suicidal thoughts, but assured me she had no intention of acting on them, as there would be no one to care for her twelve-year-old son.

This time we used the Emotional Shifting Process, which I had told her about earlier. I enlisted Massage Therapist, Carol Martin to assist. During our first E.S.P. session, Connie described her depression as a "physical sensation." She described it as "a twisted rubber thing" between her ears. The I.D. determined the difficulty could be traced to the age of five. Connie told us her depression began as a result of her father's unwillingness to make any time for her as a child. Connie's relationship with her father left her with an intense sense of loneliness.

In her mind's eye, Connie saw herself as a five-year-old, asking her father to play, and hearing his reply, "You need to go play somewhere else." She also recalled that, as a little girl, she would hide behind the banister of the stairway in the hall outside his study. She would contort her body so that she could see him, but he could not see her. Sometimes, she would wait for hours, just watching him.

The story of the little girl alone in the hallway offered me the opportunity to address the issue of abandonment. Edgar's death reawakened the feelings of being left alone. Connie's own inner child felt forsaken once again.

During his life, Edgar provided for his wife both emotionally and financially. When he died, she felt deserted and alone. When I asked Connie if Edgar was still present, she said he was.

"Perhaps," I suggested, "it's time for Edgar to go." However, the little-girl part of Connie was not yet prepared to release him. I wondered aloud if she could see further into the "unseen" world. She responded indeed, she could, and there were many spirits. I suggested that she try to find a spirit she liked better than the others. She said a spirit named Rachel appeared to be sweet and kind. "Perhaps Rachel could take care of the little girl," I prompted, "while Edgar journeys to the other side." Although difficult, Connie was able to surrender to her deepest emotions. She wept copiously as she told Edgar she loved him and said her good-byes.

"Before you go, Edgar," I inquired, "Do you believe in reincarnation now?" I asked. At this, Connie, Carol and I all laughed heartily. Connie reported that in her inner view, Edgar did too. In her mind's eye, she saw him glide ever so gently upwards, into the light, where she watched his sister and father greet him warmly.

As we ended the session, Connie said, "There is one more thing I want you to know." She paused briefly and added, "Edgar sent me to you." When I asked her how, she told me that following Edgar's death, as she cleaned out his desk, my business card had been the first thing she found. She believed it to be an omen, a clear message for her to see me for therapy.

In each of these case histories, something profound occurred, not only for my patients, but also for me. Did we communicate with the departed? I, frankly, do not feel I am in a position to judge with any degree of certainty. My primary concern is easing the suffering my patients feel. From my perspective, the degree to which their experiences can be considered "real" depends on our success in achieving our therapeutic goals.

10. KARMA AND REINCARNATION

"The wise grieve neither for the living nor for the dead.
There was never a time when you and I and all the
kings gathered here have not existed and nor will
there be a time when we will cease to exist."
–Anonymous, The Bhagavad Gita

When I began exploring transpersonal psychology, I was like a kid in a candy store. While I wanted to partake of all the treats, I really didn't know one from another. After being introduced to Past Life Regression Therapy by hypnotist Jim Meade in Phoenix, Arizona in 1991, and then being powerfully encouraged to pursue the technique by psychiatrist and author, Dr. Brian Weiss, I wanted to know more.

One of the paradoxes of past-life regression therapy is the phenomenon may be simple to access, but decidedly more difficult to prove the authenticity of the material. Dr. Ian Stevenson, a psychiatrist at the University of Virginia, studied the spontaneous recall of past lifetimes by children. His research documented significant correlations between physical manifestations, such as birthmarks, and the manner of death the children described.

In Stevenson's view, hypnotic regressions do not evoke "real" past lifetimes, but are artifacts of the activity of the subconscious mind. My intention is not to prove or disprove the historical accuracy of material accessed through regression. My interest lies in how this process may help to diminish emotional and physical pain. I have been impressed by the degree of emotional authenticity that accompanies many past-life regression experiences.

Two ideas integral to any understanding of past-life regression therapy are karma and reincarnation. Karma, a Sanskrit word meaning "action," is a poorly understood concept in the Western world. The law of karma ensures all individuals will have the opportunity to experience the effects of their conduct. It therefore "guarantees" all our behaviors have meaning, significance, and ultimately, repercussions.

Perhaps the best definition of karma was stated by the man often considered America's greatest psychic, "The Sleeping Prophet," Edgar Cayce. Cayce said (from trance), "Karma is meeting the self." The greatest gift given by information gleaned from examining a previous incarnation is an illumination of the present, providing new perspectives, insights, and awareness. In theory, when we change the way we live our lives, our karma changes, as well.

A common Western misconception regards karma as punishment for past misdeeds. The law of karma implies every action or inaction we have ever taken, or not taken, has an effect. Due to the repercussions of our conduct or sins of omission, we choose the conditions of incarnation with the best potential for bringing us along on a path to be closer to God. The goal is purification in love of our souls.

We are not here to pay back or to be paid back. We are here to grow. In our willingness to grow, karmic ties are released. Whether change takes several lifetimes, or only a moment, is not the most significant part of the process. Life may be seen as a schoolroom, and some of the lessons need to be so strong they are written across the heavens in order for them to be heard and understood. If we learn the lessons, become more centered in, and motivated by love, we then have the opportunity to purify ourselves and live more in resonance with a higher power.

Karma and reincarnation are related, in that karma supplies the energy resulting in reincarnation. The latter term simply refers to the idea that an individual soul may be reborn many times, into multiple bodies, living different lives during different eras.

While concepts of karma and reincarnation are central themes for a significant number of Eastern religions, they have also been identified in Judeo-Christian thought. The Kabbalah, a collection of Hebrew mystical writings, contains numerous references to 'gilgul,' or the transmigration of souls. Some sects of Judaism have embraced the concept of reincarnation for over a thousand years.

Author Stephen Lampe documented that reincarnation was included in early Christian liturgy. Christian writings found in Upper Egypt in 1945 indicates a relationship exists between the concept of reincarnation and the Christian faith. The mystical writers of these texts, known as Christian Gnostics, described what is believed to be the secret teachings of Jesus. Origen, 182-253 A.D. of Alexandria, Egypt, attempted to bring the wisdom of the Gnostics to the liturgy. Hundreds of years later, he was accused of being a heretic for his efforts. The connection between reincarnation and Christianity ended in the fourth century when Christianity was adopted as the official religion of the Roman Empire. It wasn't until the sixth century that the concept of reincarnation was theologically considered heresy by the Church. However, as late as the twelfth century, some Christian sects continued to maintain and teach a belief in reincarnation.

Part of the majesty of the subconscious mind is that it does not have boundaries of time, space, or the laws of conventional logic. In the instant of a thought, we can access other times, other places on earth, or anywhere in the universe.

As a child, I used to lie awake at night and contemplate. One of the questions to which my young mind sought an answer was, "What is the nature of time?" One night, I came to a realization; time is a circle having no beginning or end. My conception of time was different from most Western societies. Many years passed before I would learn the Western view of time is linear, in contrast to the manner how time is understood in the East (and by Native Americans), which is circular.

In western cultures, we generally think of time

as moving in an orderly, lawful fashion. Yesterday occurs before today, and today precedes tomorrow. Westerners generally also make the assumption time is divided into equal segments, in which units designated as seconds, minutes, hours, and days are the same length for everyone in every part of the universe. Although we commonly subscribe to the notion that time is orderly and lawful, our perception of time is by no means uniform. Exciting events appear to occur quickly, yet circumstances we experience as boring seem to take forever.

From the perspective of ancient mysticism in many faiths, the past, the present, and the future all exist simultaneously (in the now). For the mystic, time is considered to be part of the creative process of life, and perceived as a useful convenience for those of us here on earth, but of no essence in the higher realms.

Amazingly, some aspects of modern physics relating to time are beginning to bear a startling resemblance to ancient mysticism. In 2011, a NASA experiment confirmed Einstein's theory of space-time, showing that clocks operate differently at different points in orbit around the earth than they do on the ground.

I utilize the idea of past lives in the service of clinical improvement in my patients. I leave the task of proving the existence of past lives to those whose primary orientation is research, rather than the provision of treatment. Whether the material presenting itself during regression is "real" or "metaphorical" matters less to me than whether such information is beneficial for the patient. My primary concern is the meaning the patient ascribes to the experience. Patients report a wide range of responses within this phenomenon. While some relate that their inner perceptions feel like facts, other individuals view their experience more metaphorically.

A past-life regression can be accessed through hypnosis, as well as, the Emotional Shifting Process. The ease of access in past-life regression belies the skill required for effective healing. The actual recounting of the past lifetime only constitutes a beginning of the actual therapeutic work. The major portions of the process often occur through developing an insight into how the material that emerges reflects the current circumstances of the patient.

Linda's Southern Lifetime

Linda, a forty-nine-year-old nurse, reported she suffered from anxiety attacks. She was an unusually good hypnotic subject. Through ideo-motor signaling, she indicated her problem had its point of origin in a past lifetime. Having been reared in the Midwestern United States, Linda ordinarily spoke with the identifiable twang frequently found in the speech patterns of people from that region of the country. However, during her regression, her speech sounded distinctly Southern, and the following conversation ensued:

Linda: "It's 1822, and I live in Savannah, Georgia. My name is Rena Mae. Rena Mae Jeffries. My husband's name is Harold."

RS: "What does Harold do for a living?"

Linda: "He raises rice."

RS: "Do you have children?"

Linda: "I have a daughter, Melanie. She is seven.

She plays the piano. My father died two months ago."

RS: "Do you have servants?"

Linda: (a puzzled or mildly annoyed look on her face) "Servants? Of course!"

RS: "What happens next?"

Linda: "I'm walking by a stream. It's raining very hard. Oh my God, Melanie fell. I have to run to get her. I've got her out of the water, pushed her out of the water, but can't get myself out. If I could only get these clothes off. I'm under the water. Now I'm lookin' at my body under the water. I look up above me and see my mama. Mama's telling me to come with her. My baby is safe. So I go with my mama. We're going toward the light. Blue, bright, very pretty, pretty blue..."

In her inner vision of that lifetime, Linda saw people standing nearby who could have saved her, but she could not go to them for help, and as a result, she perished. At this realization, she acknowledged that giving others permission to help, and seeking help when needed, were indeed significant issues in the present.

The change in Linda's accent, as well as the pattern of her speech were most impressive to me. In addition, her reactions to my questions were congruent with those of the genteel wife of a Southern plantation owner of 1822.

George: The Roman General Meets Jesus

George, a physician from Canada, shared with me he wanted to be more loving to others and more open to accept their love fully. He said he had a feeling as if a a shield covered his heart. Initially a hypnotic approach was attempted, but George disengaged from the process just as he was about to access a deeply relaxed state. For our second session, he agreed to use the Emotional Shifting Process. Massage Therapist, Carol Martin, assisted.

The Information Detector (I.D.) indicated the point of origin of George's "shield" was a past lifetime. George saw himself as a Roman soldier of high standing, wearing a protective breastplate. "I'm a General," he said. "I bring fear to the people, both with my authority as a general and powerful physique." He saw himself in ancient Israel during the time of Jesus. George described a chance meeting with members of the Essene sect. He became extremely emotional when he acknowledged that among the members of this group was Jesus. This contact created much inner conflict for the Roman military man. To maintain his position of power in the brutal business of war, the General had to detach himself from the feelings of others. He could not afford the luxury of feeling empathy for those in the armies he opposed or lands he occupied. When George began to realize the General had no real love for himself, his heart began to open. He felt pain and heaviness in his chest.

The encounter with Jesus altered everything for George. As a General, he could not make the leap from being Roman to being Christian. He felt as if he had been stripped naked of all that insulated him for so long. The internal turmoil was so resistant to resolution, so painful, that ultimately, in depression and despair, the General hurled himself upon his sword and died. The patient's chest swelled and heaved as he sobbed uncontrollably. His body released the energy that had been held hostage by this conflict throughout his life.

After the session, George addressed the need to experience more compassion for himself as a caring physician, for the patients he helped, and even for the General in ancient Rome. "Imagine the choice with which the General was faced," he said. "If he allowed himself to feel, he would lose everything he had built in the physical and material world. In the very act of allowing himself his feelings, he would gain the sense of inner peace that comes with spirituality."

At the completion of our session, there was softness in George's face and eyes I had not seen before. He conferred the warmest of heartfelt hugs upon us. He confided he had been searching for many years for a process to help him open his heart. I was deeply and profoundly touched by the genuineness and authenticity of emotion he expressed during the experience. It was my privilege to be present as his heart unfolded.

Rhonda At Gettysburg

Rhonda, a nurse whom I met while presenting a workshop on past-life regression therapy, told me about a resistant, troublesome symptom that had been bothering her for over a year. Rhonda suffered from intense migraine headaches after exposure to the color red. If she walked into a room with a red carpet, it would likely initiate a severe headache. She agreed to work with the Emotional Shifting Process with Physical Therapist, Grace Walters.

Although Rhonda experienced no relief from

her headaches as a result of our initial session, she continued to be optimistic about the potential for healing. When we met for our second session about three weeks later, I.D. indicated the point of origin of her symptoms was before birth. With little encouragement, she quickly accessed a past lifetime. She then began to speak in a somewhat disjointed manner, almost as if she were in shock. "I'm outside," she said. "Its a fight, a battle. Soldiers. I'm a woman. Bring in the wounded. I'm a nurse during the Civil War. The people that are hurt are boys, young boys. There are cannons."

She paused, then continued her description of the scene emerging from within. "They drag them to a place where there are a lot of boys. There's a doctor. I can't believe they're hurt so bad. He tells me who I should fix and leave the others for dead. They're bleeding everywhere. It's terrible. There are so many dead. We can't help them all. I don't have enough bandages. He says, 'Never mind. They're going to die anyway.' It feels hopeless. There are just so many bodies." I ask him, "What are we going to do with the dead? What about their families?" He says, 'We'll worry about that later, there are too many.'"

Rhonda continued on. "I have a brother here somewhere," she exclaimed. "I'm worried he's dead, too. We will never find him. There are so many bodies with huge holes in them." After she had expressed the emotion related to the scene in her mind's eye, I asked what she thought the lesson to be learned from this lifetime might be. She paused reflectively for a moment before answering, "There are times when, no matter what you do, you can't fix something," she intoned. "Do what you are able and the rest will take care of itself." At the conclusion of our session, Rhonda offered an additional comment, "I don't like visiting Civil War battlefields," she mused, "because it seems as if I am always able to hear the battle."

When Rhonda returned approximately one month later for a follow-up session, she happily reported she had experienced only one mild headache since her E.S.P. session and past-life regression. "I went to the movies," she told me excitedly. I didn't understand the meaning of this statement, until she explained she had been afraid of the red carpets so many theaters have in their lobbies. She said, "I guess it reminded me of all that blood on the ground in Gettysburg."

Bill's Warrior Life

Bill suffered from anxiety that began more than five years before our meeting, after he left a job as an elementary school teacher to study physical therapy. One of Bill's clinical rotations placed him at a general hospital, where his first panic attack occurred.

He related that he had been walking past the critical care unit when he became dizzy and breathless. His heart rate increased rapidly, and his physical symptoms were accompanied by the terrifying thought he was having a heart attack. Bill had the presence of mind to sit down right where he was and to take deep breaths. The episode soon passed. Later, he went to see his physician, who was unable to detect anything wrong with his heart.

Initially, Bill perceived the anxiety as a one-time

thing and readily dismissed it. This truly was the case until after his graduation, when he got a job in a hospital. However, shortly after beginning his new job, the anxiety attacks re-emerged, quickly increasing in frequency to three times a day. The experiences were so debilitating, it wasn't long before he left his job. Bill sought the help of a psychotherapist and a psychiatrist, where he received limited relief. He was placed on anti-anxiety medication, but it only helped a little.

When I met Bill, it was obvious he was hesitant to open up about something, "I heard about you from a friend. I think you can help me. I think my problems are from . . . before." When I asked him what he meant, he explained he had memories of a lifetime that was not his own. I reassured him I would work hard to help him resolve his problem, wherever its origin. I explained to him the advantage of having a body therapist in the session. Desperate to get over his anxiety, he readily agreed. Carol Martin helped me with Bill.

The I.D. indicated the point of origin of the problem was at age two. Bill claimed to have retained some memories of that time in his life, but couldn't fathom why there would be so much anxiety generated during that period of time, as he could recall nothing memorable.

I, too, was puzzled and went over the material several times with Bill, but each time the same answer was manifested. The I.D. repeatedly indicated age two was significant, but our exploration of that time uncovered little that seemed relevant. I decided to try a different approach. I inquired, "Does the two-year-old hold significant memories of a past lifetime?" I.D. indicated yes, and Bill immediately began to access his anxiety.

"I feel cold." He shivered. "My body is tingling."

Bill's face became clenched tighter than a fist. He began to grunt and groan in pain. With his jaw now jutting out, he growled, "Something is cutting me," and pointed with his right index finger to a place just below his neck. "What does it feel like?" I asked. He started to shake on the table. His body suddenly lurched up from a supine position to a sitting one. "I don't know," he replied, "I think it's my imagination."

"I want you to use your imagination, Bill," I encouraged. "Your body will tell us if you get off track," I had to raise my voice to be heard over his loud moaning.

"It's got to be a spear or a lance or something," his booming voice declared. "I can taste the blood in my mouth. I can feel the metal spear in my body." Bill began to become quiet, "I'm dying," he sobbed. "I have failed." "Bill, what are you feeling?" I inquired. He clenched even tighter in response to this query. Then he relaxed slightly and sighed, "This guy is absolutely furious." "What does the anger get you?" I asked. "The anger keeps me alive. It helps me survive," Bill replied. I had the uncanny sensation I was speaking directly to a wounded warrior.

"I'm not afraid of death, but I hate to lose," he stated. "I hate to lose," he reiterated. As Bill spoke, his midsection began to shake wildly, as the emotional energy was released and flowed from his body. His voice became weak. It was apparent to me the warrior who he had been was in his death throes. "I am not afraid to die, but I really do not like to lose," he repeated his earlier message. His body, as well as his vocalizations, became quieter and quieter, until he was completely still.

"Warrior," I asked. "Do you have any advice for Bill?" He laughed gently. "Duck the spear next time," he replied. I spoke to him in the softest voice I could muster, "Warrior, the anger may have kept you alive, but it can be very harmful to Bill. He needs your strength, cunning, skill, persistence, and valor, but fury is destructive to him. You were enraged at your loss, but if you are here now, what did you really lose?" Bill came out of the session feeling cold and shaky. He wondered aloud if this was all his imagination or if something had really happened.

At our next session, when I peered into the waiting room to invite him in, I found Bill in the middle of an anxiety attack. He was sweating, clammy, nervous, and shaking. He asked me if this was a good time to work on himself. I felt his dramatic presentation of symptoms represented a golden opportunity for healing. As soon as Bill lay down on the therapeutic table, Carol identified birth as the point of origin of the current anxiety attack.

Bill related he had been adopted as a very young child. He did not have any contact with his biological mother following his birth. As such, he was unable to detail any emotional events of his birth, other than speculating his mother may have been very frightened.

He then reported that anxiety had begun to course down the center of his body. As it did so, Bill related he was beginning to feel cold in his hands and feet. I gently questioned him about his feelings. In a quiet voice he talked about a great sense of loneliness and sadness surrounding his birth.

I asked him to look inside his body to view these feelings. He said, "I see a small black spot, the shape of a heart, in my heart." I offered a long pillow, then suggested he hold it close to his body and imagine himself being held and loved by his mother. While silent tears streamed down his cheeks , Bill expressed a great deal of sadness. We then discussed some positive qualities he gained from imagining his birth experience. He identified the understanding of pain as something important to his work.

Abruptly, without warning, his jaw stuck out. and he started to grunt and groan as though in pain. Simultaneously, his body began to duplicate the serpentine movements similar to a baby coming down the birth canal. Bill finished his journey through "delivery" with a lot of emotion and physical releases. At the end of the session he said he felt stronger and calmer than he could ever remember. Bill continued conventional therapy with me for another month during which had no further anxiety issues. He has since entered a program to become a licensed mental health counselor and reported he was coping well with the rigors of being a student again.

The Emotional Shifting Process allows access to powerful information that helps people move forward in their emotional growth. For some, the inner story involves a past lifetime. I do not judge the metaphors that represent the deepest motivations of an individual's life path. My job is to support each individual's healing journey. I respect the patient's process, no matter how far into the past we have to go to find the origin of symptoms.

11. SPIRIT

"We shall not cease from exploration
And the end of all our exploring
Will be to arrive where we started
And know the place for the first time."
–T.S. Eliot

"In the end, it's all about spirit."
–Richard G. Schulman, PhD and many others.

Spiritual experiences can manifest in a variety of ways: through dreams, voices, bodily sensations, visions, or an intuitive insight. Any and all of these uncanny occurrences have the potential to facilitate great leaps of understanding and healing.

I think of spirituality as a means to describe the spark of God each of us carry within. It's the capability everyone has of experiencing the healing effects of a direct encounter with the divine. Manifestations range from sublime phenomena, such as visions of angels, to the simplicity of deriving deeper meaning from a life event.

Spirituality involves the belief that forces beyond the physical and material influence our perceptions, thoughts, attitudes, feelings, and behavior accompanying life circumstances. Spirituality can significantly impact the outcome of any given situation. Spiritual forces involve precognition, clairvoyance, conversing with guides and angels, out of body and near death experiences, powerful dream states, and numerous other marvelous experiences that bespeak the presence of a rich inner landscape.

Claire Leaves Her Body

Claire was a chronic pain patient who worked with me for several months following a car accident. Utilizing conventional psychotherapy, physical therapy, chiropractic, and massage in the course of her rehabilitation, she made a recovery that was both steady and admirable. After a period of months, she was able to manage her pain to the extent that she could resume working full-time. But she continued to feel "haunted" by the accident and decided to address this discomfort. Massage Therapist, Carol Martin, joined me for our work with Claire using the Emotional Shifting Process.

Claire's intuitive feelings directed us to start our exploration at the point of her accident. Out of the corner of her eye, she saw a car carrying a young woman and two young children change lanes, and another vehicle with an older woman unexpectedly pull out into the same lane. The car driven by the young woman, in an attempt to avoid striking the second vehicle, careened toward Claire. The next thing Claire knew, she was outside her car and comforting the two children.

I asked her to review the accident again, carefully and slowly. As she did so, Carol monitored the I.D. Shortly, she told me the moment of impact of the other car on Claire's vehicle was particularly significant. I encouraged Claire once again to see the accident in her mind. Each time she engaged the memory, Claire remembered greater detail. Finally, on the fourth repetition, she excitedly exclaimed, "I see her face sideways. I couldn't have seen it like that unless I was outside the car."

When I asked her to describe the moment of impact, she calmly replied, "I know the feelings of the children in the car. I can feel their fear. I am telling them not to worry." Having heard her own words, she was silent for a moment. Then she intoned, "Here comes the White Light."

At this point, her back became rigid and uncomfortable. The reappearance of these symptoms led me to believe important material was still in the process of unfolding. I requested she return in her mind to the moment of impact once again. She could hear the screams of the children. As she braced herself against the steering wheel, she was buffeted by the tremendous force of the impact. Spontaneously, she related she was beginning to see the White Light in her field of view once again. "I h-have to save those ch-children," she stammered. "The children are all right," I assured her, "but you are not. Who will take care of you?" "I'm okay," she protested.

I reminded her that if she had been so "okay," it

is highly unlikely she would have a period of many months in pain and treatment. "Your injuries are far worse than anyone else's," I said, "and it is now time for you to take care of yourself. Please bring healing into your body." Within moments, she began to relax. She then began to talk about her newfound need to accept her own healing abilities.

A few months later, Claire decided to leave her job and go back to school, with the intention of becoming a physician. She is currently in medical school, and recently wrote to say she was doing well.

Wendy's Psychic Intuition

The next case involved a person who needed to accept her powerful intuitive gifts and ability to access the spirit world to heal her flying phobia. Wendy, a twenty-nine-year-old, single woman with blond, curly hair and blue eyes, entered therapy due to her fear of flying. Her fears threatened a planned vacation to Europe. Massage Therapist, Carol Martin worked with me.

Wendy lay on the therapeutic table. Once Carol touched her shoulder and we began the therapy session, she quickly reached a deeply relaxed state. I suggested to her subconscious mind that it lead her to the point of origin of her anxiety. Wendy saw herself in an airport some nine years before. She was preparing to embark on a flight from Boston, her hometown, to Florida. Carol Martin nodded her head "Yes" indicating that the I.D. was in agreement with Wendy's report.

Wendy said she felt queasy as soon as the picture

of the airport appeared in her mind's eye. When she viewed herself near the ticket agent, her nausea increased. Once she saw herself on the plane, all emotion shut down. She felt as if she had been anesthetized, as if she was completely numb.

I advanced Wendy in time by one hour. She told me the feeling in her stomach had now progressed to a severe state of nausea. I then suggested she activate the point of origin of the nausea. Wendy began to speak softly, as if from a dream. Barely audible, she whispered, "I can see fluid leaking out of the wing on my side of the plane. The stewardess is handing me a pillow, telling everyone how to sit during a crash landing." Upon hearing her own words, Wendy's body began to shake in her chair.

She started to sob. As her tears flowed, she acknowledged, "I know what those feelings were in my stomach. They were premonitions that I shouldn't get on that plane." I encouraged her to move through the remainder of the flight. In her mind's eye, she confronted her fear of death as the craft hurtled toward the ground. Fortunately the pilot landed the plane safely, and no one was hurt. Wendy had apparently experienced multiple premonitions telling her the aircraft was going to encounter trouble. She ignored all of them. In so doing, she had prevented her intuitive self from informing her of the danger she faced.

I asked her to get back in touch with her intuitive self regarding her upcoming flight. She happily stated the nausea had vanished. She felt sure she would have a wonderful time in Europe. Some weeks later, she informed me her trip had been more enjoyable than she anticipated, and she actually appreciated the flight.

Iris' Holocaust Life and Tattoo

Iris, a 36-year-old woman, changed careers to become a massage therapist. Once she started school, she felt a sense of freedom in her chosen path and decided to get a tattoo to celebrate her career change. She reported having panic attacks almost immediately after she got the tattoo. She was so upset we decided to try the Emotional Shifting Process immediately. Massage Therapist, Carol Martin agreed to assist.

Iris began to have an emotional reaction as soon as she lay down on the table. Once she calmed a bit, Carol determined the point of origin of her panic was age 11. She described her home and life at that time, but could not come up with anything that seemed to explain the high level of anxiety she was experiencing. I asked her if anything unusual had happened. She said age 11 was when she began reading about metaphysics and started playing with a Ouija Board. She said she and her friends felt like they had been communicating with spirits.

I asked if she felt like any of the spirits were still with her. She said, "Yes." Using the I.D., Carol Martin indicated this was emotionally significant. She told us her left leg, where the body art was located, felt like wood. Her anxiety was starting to ramp up again with great ferocity. I told her to let the right leg, the one she could still feel, tell her what the problem was. She said, "I can see smoke and soldiers. There are starving people in striped pajamas." She told us she was receiving a picture of the Holocaust from World War II.

At this point she began to writhe and the energy began to release. Iris said she felt something lift off her shoulders and became very serene. Iris related afterwards she was convinced a troubled spirit in her energy field had been released. Iris was happy to report her panic attacks ceased and did not return.

Dale's Inner Demon

The last case in this chapter is that of a man who thought he was possessed by a demon. He had to journey deep inside himself to find his truth. Dale was a profoundly depressed thirty-three-year-old electrician. When we met initially, he related that his marriage was crumbling and his job was tenuous, as a result of emotional turmoil. He agreed to work with Massage Therapist, Carol Martin, using the Emotional Shifting Process.

Dale had the ability to travel to the deepest reaches of his inner world almost effortlessly. He was also capable of speaking about his experiences without disturbing his level of trance. During an E.S.P. session, Dale said he could clearly see an inner light. He wondered aloud if he should move toward it. "I can see it, but there's a blemish in it," he observed hesitantly. As he began to get closer to the light, Dale spoke haltingly, "I'm afraid. I think its God... or a demon." I wanted to speak with the inner entity more directly. Leaning forward, I whispered. "Are you an angel?" After pausing for a moment, Dale, said, "Yes and no, I think it's a demon."

I encouraged Dale to imagine a powerful beam of light to illuminate the figure. Upon doing so, he announced that the demon appeared to be shrinking and trying to hide.

I told Dale to move around to the other side of the demon and to shine even more light on it, but he couldn't. "It ran into the fog," he muttered. "Now I'll never find it."

I then suggested he imagine a large electric fan, one that was easily capable of blowing the fog away. Once he indicated that the fog had dissipated, I confronted the demon. "Tell me who you are," I demanded. "I remember him from when I was a kid," Dale intervened, "something like him was always telling me I was bad, that I was evil." "Tell me who you are," I reiterated.

Dale was perspiring and undergoing a great deal of stress. His body began to vibrate noticeably. Carol Martin placed my hand in the area of Dale's heart. I felt a discharge of energy, as if bees had flown through my hand. As the session ended, Dale spoke softly. "I know who this demon is," he allowed. "He is a little boy I created when I was a child. I think he might be a part of me."

Our following meeting began with Dale reporting a recurring nightmare, in which he dreamt an evil spirit possessed him. When I asked him to "reconnect" with the demon in his dream, he saw the figure, in his mind's eye, as a little boy about five years old. The child was dressed in a striped polo shirt and blue shorts.

Although now revealed as being flesh-and-blood, and considerably less frightening than an evil spirit, the little boy was reluctant to relinquish his rage. It was apparent to me that this little child had begun to hate himself at a very early age. His self-hatred only allowed him to bond with others who were mean to him. In so doing, he felt less isolated. Using such feelings, however negative and destructive, as a connector to others was evidently preferable for the boy than feeling alone. Dale began to realize he would do almost anything to avoid the profound feelings of loneliness he knew as a child.

At the start of our next session, Dale's affect was brighter. He reported his mood had improved. After these experiences, his difficulties, though diminished, had not been resolved. Several months later, he began to become depressed and angry again. He stated he was incensed at God. Once again, he was obsessed about the "demon."

Seeing that conventional therapy was not producing positive results, Dale asked to try the Emotional Shifting Process again. During the session, the little boy part of him was now willing to talk with me. He related he had been created during a voyage to heaven. I re-engaged the adult Dale who recalled the incident taking place during a church service when he was five years old. As he was listening to the preacher speak about heaven, he felt himself gently leaving his body, rising into the sky, and sailing effortlessly toward a bright white light. He had enjoyed a beautiful experience, after which he had drifted slowly back to the church.

Returning to the house of worship, Dale recounted that he was horrified at the sight of black shadows surrounding many of the parishioners. He then saw the scene at the church becoming "cloudy," and began to describe the molestation of a young child, which had apparently occurred in the back of the church. For the next few minutes, I strongly encouraged Dale, "Try to see through the clouds. What do you see taking place?" Despite great trepidation, he was finally able to respond. "My God," he exclaimed suddenly, "that little boy was me."

The boy who molested him was much older than he. Apparently the boy's father was an elder of the church. At first, the playfulness, and even the touching seemed like a game, but all pretense of play came to an abrupt and confusing end when the older boy insisted Dale have sex with him.

Dale became very frightened and wanted to run away. When the other boy ordered him to stay, he became frantic. His fear was so overwhelming he felt paralyzed.

As the patient lay on the therapeutic table, viewing these events through his inner vision, he reported being chased by a wall of darkness. Speaking through Dale but directly to the frightened little fellow within him, I encouraged him to run. Ultimately, he was able to outrace most of the darkness. In a flash of brilliance worthy of Dr. Carl Jung, Dale spontaneously said the darkness was the shadow of his own fear and anger,

I suggested he turn and confront his tormentor, and with great courage he found the strength to do so. Forcing himself to stare resolutely at the shadow, he was able to stop it in its tracks. As the figure stood silently anchored to the ground where it had trod so menacingly just a few moments before, Dale was able to walk past it.

The ramifications of the breakthrough Dale accomplished during this session seemed monumental. His depression began to lift. He reported a newfound ability to tolerate disappointment and his attitude changed toward himself and others. He began to make new friends and become active within the community. With steady and continued improvement, we diminished the frequency of our meetings from weekly to bi-weekly. Unexpectedly, however, Dale told me he was profoundly depressed again; and this time suicidal.

Looking at the floor as he spoke, he said, "Richard, the blackness came back. It is so bad I don't want to go on anymore. I thought we were done with that." His eyes filled with tears as he talked about the anger and frustration he was feeling, a sense that nothing had really changed.

Many months before this session, Dale had spoken bitterly about a memory he had carried from age three. He was riding in a car with his family and had fallen asleep. Upon awakening, he discovered the car had stopped and he was alone. Peering out a window, he saw his parents and brother walking toward a grocery store. He experienced terrifying feelings of abandonment.

Carol Martin confirmed that age three was the point of origin of the current depression, I remembered his statement about the pain he had experienced in the car at that time. Before I could even request the patient return to the scene, he balked.

"Sure, I can see myself in the car asleep, and alone," he announced bitterly, "but I'm not going to do it. It's the time my family left me." Although I understood why the patient would express such determined reluctance to return to so painful an experience, the I.D. had indicated it was of vital importance for him to do so. Dale finally agreed to examine the events of that day one more time.

He saw himself traveling in the family car, and then felt himself being lulled to sleep by the sound of the engine. I encouraged him to remain acutely aware of what transpired in the car as he slept. "The car just stopped," he observed, "and my mother is looking at me asleep on the back seat. Now, she's starting to speak. She's saying, 'It would be a shame to wake him up. He looks so peaceful and happy. Let's let him sleep. We'll only be gone for a few minutes, anyway.'"

In his mind's eye, the patient witnessed his mother gently and carefully put a blanket over him, after which everyone quietly and considerately exited the car. Perhaps it was the closing of one of the car doors that awakened little Dale. We will never know for certain. But, for whatever reason, he started to stir. Coming out of a deep state of sleep, he at first was quite disoriented as to where he was. He rubbed the sleep out of his eyes. When he looked about, he was terrified at finding himself alone.

At this realization, he began to panic. He stood up, and when he did, he could see his family walking away from him. As they got increasingly farther from him, he started to cry and bang on the back window of the car. Dale paused for a moment in his recollection. Indeed, this was precisely where his previous description of the events had ended, many months ago.

None of us could have anticipated what occurred next. As tears streamed down his face, Dale whispered, "My brother is coming back for me! He saw me, and he's coming back for me!" Dale went on to describe his brother Jimmy opening the door of the car, freeing him from his confinement and isolation. Hand in hand, the two brothers then caught up with the rest of the family.

Dale's body relaxed perceptibly with this new recounting of his experience. Afterwards, I considered asking him which of his two experiences was the truth, but decided against it. The darkness that was such a part of his life had given way to light. In essence, wasn't that the only truth that mattered?

I saw Dale for an additional two months to reinforce and monitor his gains. During that time, his symptoms of depression receded and appeared to resolve themselves. Six months after concluding therapy, he returned briefly to address relationship issues. At that time, he assured me that although he struggled occasionally like everyone else, he had not been revisited by the dismal depression and despair that had once been such familiar and constant companions.

12. ADDICTION AND HEALING

"Addiction is the only disease where one of the symptoms is it tells you that you don't have it."'
Mark Sylvester, MD

"Alive we can fix, dead we can't."
Chuck Madden, Addiction Coach

The phone rang as I was getting out of the shower on a Friday evening after work. The mother of one of my young patients, Jake, was screaming into the phone, "He's dead, not breathing, what do I do?" "Call 911, I'll be over as soon as I can," I replied.

I got dressed quickly and made my way over to their home. The lights of the ambulance were flashing as I turned onto the street. My body started to shake as I parked the car and saw a gurney being wheeled out the front door. I wondered if the blanket would be over his head or would I see him still alive. More on Jake later.

Perhaps as a reflection of the times, over the last few years, my practice of psychology has morphed from a general practice where addiction was an important, but secondary issue, to one in which the treatment of addiction has become a primary issue. I now deal with the causes and consequences of addiction on an almost daily basis.

Several years ago, I co-taught a course titled "Life Skills and Recovery," at a local AA meeting. This experience expanded of my already strong respect for the "Big Book" of AA, and gave a greater an awareness of the important information psychology had to offer the recovering addict to support sobriety. While teaching, I often had the feeling I was addressing 35 initiates in the search of some higher meaning in their lives.

There are two primary rules I adhere to in the treatment of addiction: Rule #1: young addicts die; Rule #2: doctors cannot change Rule #1. I consider addiction a disease as dangerous as cancer, so I take the circumstances surrounding addiction seriously every time I engage with a patient struggling with this issue. I want the recovering addict to receive biological support, whether in the form of diet, exercise, nutritional support, psychotropic medication, or a combination of any of the aforementioned. I also work with the family of the addict, when such support is available. I leave no stone unturned as I look for leverage to keep the recovering addict sober or moving the practicing addict into a state of recovery.

Information about recovery and how to work with the recovering addict is plentiful. I particularly like the model and philosophy of Terence T. Gorski, M.A., C.A.C. Gorski uses a developmental model of recovery

I find very helpful. The primary purpose of AA is to help the addict stay sober for one day. I am there to help the addict cope with his or her life, and over time have a deeper understanding of his or her self, components of physical, emotional and spiritual health, and how to neutralize triggers that lead to relapse.

When Gorski describes relapse he uses the metaphor of all the factors involved as being akin to knocking over a row of dominos. In this model, the first domino or incident is small and they get successively bigger over time. One domino or event knocks over the next and they get bigger and bigger. He states the dominos circle around until the last one hits the addict from behind. A trigger is an event most often handled well, but under certain conditions, causes the addict to snap, as stress and emotion overtake the addict's mind.

The Emotional Shifting Process is now being used effectively to identify and de-activate triggers that engage a relapse. The conventional wisdom, as well as my own experience, informs us that relapse usually begins two to four weeks prior to use of a substance, and often is connected to an emotional triggering mechanism. In my experience just identifying the trigger is not enough. We must make every effort to reduce the emotional energy connected to the trigger so it loses the power to ignite, combust, and consume a recovering addict's sobriety.

One other event has changed the landscape of the Emotional Shifting Process. Call it fate, karma, or simply good fortune. Adrienne Borden-Sundberg, Acupuncture Physician, moved into the office complex about two years ago. While she is a highly skilled acupuncture physician, I did not realize she was also an insightful and talented Medical Intuitive. She is able to visualize the body's energies as well as anyone I had ever heard of, much less met. Two of the cases illustrated in this chapter involve her wonderful skills.

Wendy: Why do I fall apart?

Wendy, a 24 year old grad student in psychology, had been clean of a pill addiction for a year, but recently relapsed. She had just completed a 28-day rehab and was referred to me for follow up treatment. She was not very keen on attending NA meetings, but grudgingly agreed to go to AA meetings as part of her recovery plan.

She saw me twice, did not show up for follow up appointments and did not respond to texts or phone messages. I accept that some patients do not connect and move on to other therapists or aren't ready to engage in therapy.

I was somewhat surprised when she called about six months later to restart her therapy. When she came in she told me the reason she stopped seeing me was her former therapists were all "interns and rookies." She realized I saw through her and wasn't comfortable with that. She related she had been molested as a young girl and had not been ready to deal with the material. I told her, the speed of the therapy was completely up to her and I would not address the trauma until she was ready.

Wendy spent a few months looking at everything

in her life except the molestation. She engaged strongly in the recovery process. She secured a good job, moved into a sober living house and attended AA meetings regularly. She began to take piano lessons, something she had loved in her childhood. Above everything else, she maintained her sobriety.

During a session, seemingly out of the blue, Wendy's eyes misted over and she inquired, "Why did I fall apart in last weeks AA meeting?" I asked her what happened. She said that someone spoke about being sexually abused in the meeting and she broke down.

I gently told her that the other person's experience resonated with hers and evoked an emotional reaction. When she seemed perplexed with that explanation, I said, "Take two pianos next to each other, play a C chord on one and the other will start to vibrate with a C chord as well." That made sense to her. I asked if she was ready to work on the trauma.

Haltingly, she said, "Yes." When I described the Emotional Shifting Process to her, she was adamant. No one was to touch her in the therapy. I decided to utilize a trauma release technique I sometimes incorporate in ESP that does not require physical touch and see if it would be enough to free her of her emotional trauma.

The next session began with Wendy sitting back in the recliner, while I asked her to engage the memory of the molestation. She had an excellent visual memory and began recounting the event. I told her, "When you hit significant anxiety, let me know." She did, and I used the eye movement technique I learned from Neuro-Linguistic Programming. With each successive moment of anxiety, we used eye movement again. At the end of her recall, I asked her to replay the entire memory once again. She looked at me with bewilderment in her eyes. "The memory seems foggy. I don't understand it, but I'm not scared of it anymore." She ended the session perplexed about what had taken place, but glad that it did.

The next week, Wendy came in looking more relaxed than I had ever seen her. She said, "I felt as if I was carrying an 80 pound pack on my back and it's gone." Soon after, she wound down her therapy. She contacted me later to report she graduated and is now on the path to become a Licensed Mental Health Counselor.

Pete: Every Six Months

Pete, a 58 year old, successful financier who had previously failed at several rehab attempts, had reached a particularly low point in his life and was desperate for change. He was a Wall Street guy who liked to win at things. His pattern over the last few years was to enter rehab, come out gung ho for recovery and AA, but after about six months, he would find himself relapsing once again.

We began working together after a significant binge. Pete was reticent to engage in the Emotional Shifting Process and there were certainly enough practical issues to be dealt with first. He moved into sober living and engaged in a program of recovery through Alcoholics Anonymous.

Over time, Pete became irritable with his circumstances. While he continued in AA, his unhappiness with his marriage and work were palpable. When we were about to hit the six-month trigger, he disappeared. I called and left messages several times, but did not receive a reply.

Three months later, Pete re-emerged, indicating he would like to begin therapy again. When we met, he described an alcoholic binge that brought him to the edge of death, not once, but twice. I told him I would take him back as a patient if, in addition to a strong AA recovery program, he would agree to participate in the Emotional Shifting Process. Desperation is often the key to an addict engaging in a powerful recovery program with a chance for success. Pete was desperate enough to agree. Accupuncture Physician and Medical Intuitive, Adrienne Borden-Sundberg, worked with me on this case.

Our first meeting uncovered a variety of physical problems that are often consequences of alcohol addiction, as well as, strong anxiety creating tightness in his chest. Adrienne suggested some natural remedies that Pete could pursue and we agreed to meet again.

In the following session, Pete spoke about unhappy times when his family moved during his grade school years and about repeatedly having to make new friends. He also discussed the loss of his first love around age 20. Neither event explained his binge drinking. However, when he spoke about experiencing a blackout while drinking at age 39, his mood darkened. Using her skills as a Medical Intuitive, Adrienne was able to gain the insight that shame was the activator of Pete's binge drinking.

It was in Pete's third session where we uncovered

the trigger to the binges. Pete related his greatest shame came when he began to drink and passed out while having the responsibility to care for his then two-year old daughter. She was not harmed, but he was horribly shamed.

Pete's body shook as he related how horrible he felt that day. He described his shame as being bigger than his body. He looked at himself as a person who did not deserve to be loved. He felt after the incident that he had to be perfect to be loved and he knew would never be perfect. I used some eye movement release techniques learned from Neuro-Linguistic Programming to help with these irrational beliefs.

We were unable to discover the reason behind the six-month lag time and it's importance to Pete's sobriety. However, he did acknowledge he had never been able to ask for help. He said he felt big changes coming. When we hit the six-month point in his sobriety, we all held our collective breath, but Pete did not drink. He did, however, become very depressed, and while continuing his psychotherapy, was referred for medication.

Pete has been sober now for over a year. He has been working on reclaiming his professional life and marriage, but mostly he is focusing on living a life of high integrity. Pete has moved back in with his wife and family. He is currently working the12 steps of a local AA program and lives a sober life.

Connor: Did That Really Happen?

Connor, a 48 year old, practicing attorney, who has homes in Florida and in Michigan, was referred for treatment of alcoholism. In the past, he had experienced significant periods of sobriety. However, over the last year, his drinking had reached extreme levels, to the point it was threatening his job and his marriage. Moreover, due to a heart condition and diabetes, his health was seriously compromised, as well.

During our initial session, I asked if he had ever been physically or sexually mistreated. He related he thought something happened with a music teacher when he was a young boy. Almost immediately, he started to sweat, looked anxious and loudly exclaimed, "I made it up, nothing happened. My parents were good people. They protected me." I gently told him, "If what you told me was true, it would explain a lot." He shut down and gave one-word answers for the rest of the interview.

I was somewhat surprised when he scheduled another appointment. He wanted to talk about many things, except the incident with the music teacher. He was very worried he would relapse, which did occur soon thereafter. He would call me while drunk, one time while sitting in his car in the parking lot of my office, and leave horribly rude messages. When he would sober up, he would apologize, and begin working in therapy again.

Connor was often angry and hostile, yet at other times he could be very witty, intelligent, and insightful. His manner was erratic, to say the least. During one session, he showed up with his wife and gave us quite a show. He was able to conceal his drunken state during the beginning of the session, but soon became verbally abusive to his wife. It was clear he was out of control. I ended the session, sent him home and told him to come back when he was sober. He had a few choice words for me upon his exit.

Not long after that event, he returned to Michigan for the summer. I couldn't get him out of my thoughts, so one day, I called his wife to see how he was doing. She was very upset. She told me Connor was on a bender, endangering his health and his job. Considering his health status, I insisted she bring him to an inpatient treatment program. She was fearful of his anger when she would confront him, but her concern for his safety won out. Sometimes, all a person needs is a little guidance, so I coached her as to how to find a rehab program and how to deal with his resistance. He was admitted within 24 hours.

When Connor returned to Florida, I agreed to work with him only if he would do deeper work, namely the Emotional Shifting Process. He was desperate enough to agree. Acupuncture Physician and Medical Intuitive, Adrienne Borden-Sundberg, worked with me on Connor.

As I related earlier, Adrienne works a little differently than the body therapists I've engaged in the Emotional Shifting Process previously mentioned. Adrienne does not want or need to know anything about a patient prior to the first session. She reads the body energies without preconceived ideas as to what she may find. I use what she discovers as hypotheses to follow up and have found her information to be uncannily accurate at targeting important areas to explore.

When she gave me her impressions regarding Connor, she was so on target that he became angry and accused me of telling her his story beforehand. Once I reassured him there was no reason for me to mislead him about our process we began to work.

I told Connor we did not have to work on the "Age Seven" hypothesis indicated by Adrienne's scan. Of course this was the age he had previously told me he was molested and immediately denied he had ever said it in our first session. We then spent three sessions working on other concerns. All of the issues we addressed in their own way funneled back to the sexual trauma at age seven.

Connor wondered why he found it so difficult to complete things. He told me he went to EMT school and dropped out just before completion. He trained as a firefighter and passed all but one of the exams and never went back to retake the final exam. In the Air Force, he was being groomed as a fighter pilot and gave up. I felt that for this man, if things were good, this brought up anxiety. He was able to see this, but had no theory as to why this would be the case.

He was very reticent to place any blame on his parents. As a rule, I do not engage in parent bashing. However, I often find it important for a patent to actually feel his or her feelings about a neglectful or abusive parent before the matter of forgiveness can be worked on.

Grudgingly, Connor admitted that his mother drank and when inebriated, she could be demanding and abusive to both he and his father. He wondered aloud why his father never stood up to her.

Adrienne indicated that age 14 held much emotional energy. Connor grinned and shook his head. "You are some kind of witch," he said. That was when I started drinking. "They wanted to control me, but no one can," he angrily exclaimed. "Anyone who tells you they didn't have a good time drinking is a liar," he went on.

I asked him how that works for him now and he became sullen and sad. "I'm losing everything. Please help me," he quietly answered.

In between the third and fourth session, Connor drank. His wife found him asleep with a large dent in the car. Connor, emerging from a blackout, had no idea what had gone on. Miraculously he did not lose his driver license, marriage, freedom, or his life.

He spoke of this event with much sadness and sense of hopelessness. I decided to turn this crisis into an opportunity. "Connor," I gently spoke. "Are you desperate?" He said, "Yes." "Good," I said. "This is the time for us to work on your trauma. You will never have a better one."

With Adrienne carefully monitoring his body's reactions, we explored his life as a seven-year old boy. He related his mother's obsession with him learning the piano. She saved up and bought an expensive piano, and engaged a music teacher.

When Connor began to talk about the music teacher, his anxiety increased dramatically. He hit the core of the trauma. He began quietly, saying how he felt uncomfortable with the teacher touching him and then burst, like an energetic atom bomb when he described being given oral sex by the teacher. His body shook violently and he cried bitterly as the energy was released.

"I couldn't tell my mother," he managed to choke out from his release. "I told her I didn't want the lessons anymore. She became furious with me. I had to go back, and each time it was worse," he sobbed.

Finally, Connor managed to tell his father, who ended the lessons. Connor's body continued to lurch back and forth on the table, but eventually, the emotional storm began to end. He looked up at me. "Are you sure I didn't make it up?" he asked. "I'm 100% positive. No one has a reaction like you did without a reason. If anything, I think you minimized what happened," I responded.

The session opened a new world for Connor. He now understood how the experience of sexual pleasure under conditions of high anxiety impacted his life, i.e. why he didn't complete things that would be good for him or that he enjoyed. He worked diligently on the idea that good is good.

Connor was set to go back to Michigan for the summer. He left me with the thought, "You know, Doc. Alcohol was the only thing I could just feel good about. I think in the end, it was because I knew it would wind up making me feel bad."

I spoke with Connor recently and while he struggles at times, he has managed to maintain his sobriety for now. He continues attending AA and sees a therapist when in Michigan. One day at a time, my friend.

Alive We Can Fix, Dead We Can't

Now back to Jake's story. Thankfully, when I saw the gurney, I saw my patient with an oxygen mask over his head. He was alive. At the insistence of his physician, Dr. Sylvester, his family had Narcan on hand. His parents were able to inject it, buying enough time for the EMT's to arrive and resuscitate him. I spent some time with the family and then went with them to the Emergency Room.

We were ushered into the room where Jake was affixed with tubes and wires both keeping him alive and letting us know his heart was still beating. As I looked around the room into the faces of his family, along with Chuck Madden, Jake's addiction coach and friend, I saw horror, as if we had all been through a terrorist attack and had somehow survived.

Jake stirred. I happened to be on his right side by the bed. He looked up groggily and saw a brace on my hand from a recent sports injury. His blue eyes focused and the first words out of his mouth were, "Richard, what happened to your hand? Are you okay?" As I held his hand in mine, my eyes filled with tears. This was the boy I was fighting so hard to save. The young man whose primary concern upon waking wasn't for himself, but for someone else.

He went in and out of consciousness that night. When it was clear that Jake was stabilized, Chuck was preparing to leave, but before doing so, he took me aside and whispered, "Alive we can fix, dead we can't."

The family began to leave, but Jake's father remained. I felt I had to stay with him. I made the excuse that I wanted to speak with the attending physician, but in reality, I felt the need to be in solidarity with this father. I silently thanked God that my children were safe. But for the grace of something higher, we might be in opposing situations.

Jake made it through the night. I wish I could say that everything was wonderful, but his road has been a rocky one. He had some Emotional Shifting Process sessions, but we were unable to target any specific trauma. Perhaps he was using more than anyone knew and this interfered with our ability to connect with whatever was going on underneath the surface. Addicts are masters of deceit. Still, even with all the chaos that has ensued in the interim, Jake is still alive, so we take things one day at a time.

The Emotional Shifting Process paired with Adrienne's wonderful intuitive gifts and knowledge of Traditional Chinese Medicine has provided me with inspiration that, given time and persistence, will enable us to learn how to help recovering addicts live a life affirming, substance free life.

EPILOGUE

"All I have is a voice
to undo the folded lie."
–W.H. Auden

We have arrived at the center of the Labyrinth, the core of the journey. Soon it will be time to move back through the path we entered upon and go back out into the world, with a new perspective, a more complete view of ourselves and the healing process.

Throughout this book, you have read about people who have experienced successful outcomes in their therapy. Some cases do not have as positive a conclusion as those presented in these pages. The practice of the healing arts does not lend itself to perfection.

For some individuals, symptoms may have a hidden utility. Retaining a symptom may be perceived consciously or unconsciously. We refer to this as secondary gain. Symptoms may serve the purpose of eliciting sympathy, lowering the expectations of others, manipulating others to do extra work, and other seemingly beneficial advantages. Under such circumstances, the identification and acceptance of secondary gain are probably as much as can be achieved. Care must be taken by the practitioner not to place blame on the patient. The most basic foundation of all healing endeavors is, "Above all else, do no harm."

Within this context, those who practice emotional release techniques must remember that emotional injury, not merely discomfort of a physical nature, still constitutes harm. Any modality that promotes the possibility of healing will also have the potential to perpetuate or even create pain. The beliefs some entertain that "everything will always turn out for the highest good," may be employed as a euphemism for not using power responsibly and wisely.

The concept "Do no harm" serves as a safeguard for the patient. It also serves as the most significant ethical criteria for the professional. Use of this concept benefits both patient and professional, as the practice of healing is facilitated by a positive and trusting interaction between the participants in relation to one another.

As a young intern at the Palo Alto Veterans Administration Medical Center, I met a patient who was very bright and, at times, remarkably insightful about himself and the events around him. Unfortunately, at other times, he was severely disturbed. Sitting with him in my tiny office, practically huddled together during our meetings, I often thought, "But for the grace of God, he and I could be in the exact opposite positions."

After several therapy sessions with this patient, I was the recipient of a most illuminating dream. In that dream, I found myself sitting with my very intelligent, psychotic patient in a sparsely furnished, almost austere room. "How silly of you to think that two people could be in a room," a voice intoned, "and only one of them would change."

A few years later, I had my first transpersonal experience. While still early in my journey, I worked with a woman who had some profound spiritual experiences during our sessions. She connected with spiritual guides, reviewed past lives, had remarkable physical healings, and looked deeply at her soul's journey in her present lifetime. At one point, she seemed to become stuck in her progress. I asked her subconscious to consider, "What are the lessons she needs to learn to move forward?" I was stunned to hear a male-sounding voice come through her saying, "These lessons are for you, not her."

In retrospect, my own transformation through the experience of practicing psychotherapy is both considerable and undeniable. Most assuredly, the changes I have undergone have been as demonstrable as that of many of my patients. At each point along the way, I found myself coping with metaphors and symbols that were new to my experience, and beyond anything I had encountered in my training. I frequently consulted therapists and healers with experience in metaphysics, bodywork, hypnosis, and other forms of transpersonal psychology, but in the end, I had to make sense and integrate everything I learned.

Each one of these ways of looking at consciousness and healing was like a precious jewel. I used them with great care in service of the patient's needs. Then one day, unbidden, everything came together. I no longer required an exotic way of looking at human experience. All of the unique and amazing experiences had been integrated in my own psyche. They made sense to me as the simple majesty of the human heart and continue to do so.

The "truth" is the fabric with which we may mend the tapestry of our souls. And whether or not we realize it, we already possess much of this truth within our own hearts. We can meet the most basic aspirations of our souls, our desire to become whole as individuals, as well as, bond and form alliances with others. Once we have accomplished this to a reasonable degree, it becomes easier for us to experience healthier relationships along with the peace of a higher spiritual life.

My yoga teacher would say the most difficult pose is rolling out the mat for practice. I am grateful to every patient who has the courage to walk through the door and trust me to guide their journey of healing, as well as, the body therapists who support the process. I must also express appreciation to you, the readers of this book, who, in essence, journeyed with us on this less traveled path.

Our society is undergoing a time of difficult shifts in the way we experience the world. Perhaps the deepest wound is the emotional devastation and spiritual longing felt by many. It is my wish the ideas presented in this book will inspire individuals to find peace and love as they seek healing at the deepest levels.

Now is the time for us to return from the Labyrinth of Healing into our families, communities, countries and our world. We must bring our transformation of wholeness to all we touch.

Peace

APPENDIX A

A STUDY OF THE EMOTIONAL SHIFTING PROCESS

Several years ago I ran an anonymous study of patients who had participated in what we then called 'the body psychotherapy team approach', now known as the Emotional Shifting Process. Due to the fact that this approach was so radically different, I decided to run a small research project to determine if it was effective.

Questionnaires were mailed to 180 patients who had experienced The Emotional Shifting Process at least twice. Patient identifying information was age and gender. The questionnaires were coded as to severity of symptoms based on the GAF (Global Assessment of Functioning) codes in the DSM-IV (Diagnostic and Statistical Manual, Forth Edition). Overall 65 questionnaires were returned.

Here are some results:

THE BODY PSYCHOTHERAPY TEAM EFFECTIVENESS

Patients were asked to rate 11 statements on a 1-7 scale.

1 = Strongly Disagree

2 = Moderately Disagree

3 = Mildly Disagree

4 = Neutral

5 = Mildly Agree

6 = Moderately Agree

7 = Strongly Agree.

1. The body psychotherapy team approach was effective in reducing my symptoms:

6.28 (Moderately to Strongly Agree)

2. The body psychotherapy team approach accessed emotional material quickly and powerfully:

6.58 (Moderately to Strongly Agree)

3. The body psychotherapy team approach helped me to release emotional blocks:

6.31 (Moderately to Strongly Agree)

4. The body psychotherapy team approach helped me to integrate emotional material:

6.21 (Moderately to Strongly Agree)

5. The body psychotherapy team approach is a good complement to conventional psychotherapy:

6.33 (Moderately to Strongly Agree)

6. The body psychotherapy team approach is a good complement to other forms of body work:

6.12 (Moderately to Strongly Agree)

7. The body psychotherapy team approach allowed me to reach emotional places I had never been able to reach with other forms of healing:

5.95 (Mildly to Moderately Agree)

8. The body psychotherapy team approach improved my relationships with loved ones:

5.80 (Mildly to Moderately Agree)

9. The body psychotherapy team approach helped me to work on psycho-spiritual issues:

5.93 (Mildly to Moderately Agree)

10. The body psychotherapy team approach is cost effective:

5.54 (Mildly to Moderately Agree)

11. I would recommend the body psychotherapy team approach to a friend or family member:

6.51 (Moderately to Strongly Agree)

SYMPTOM RELIEF

Patients were asked: "Please rate the intensity of your symptoms on a 0-100 scale(0 = no problem, 100 = the worst you could imagine)"

Beginning of Treatment	End of Treatment	% Change
Anxiety (N =44) 67.84	20.62	70% decrease
Depression (N =39)63.00	17.00	73% decrease
Anger (N =39) 66.97	19.23	71% decrease
Pain (N =14) 64.64	39.64	39% decrease

This is not a controlled, rigorous scientific study. However, for a psychotherapy study by one private practitioner, this project represents powerful evidence that something unique happened. As a psychotherapist, I believe the strongest evidence for the efficacy of the approach is the very high agreement with the statement "I would recommend the body psychotherapy team approach to a friend or family member." High agreement with that statement indicates trust in a process.

APPENDIX B:
PATIENT REACTIONS

PATIENT COMMENTS ON
EMOTIONAL SHIFTING PROCESS

"My experience with this approach has helped me a great deal. I've worked through my issues a lot faster than the conventional way. You can talk to a psychologist and I have done that route, but I was not able to get unstuck until I did the physical work. I have more courage, self-esteem, but the best thing is I don't hold on to my stuff and I"m standing up to people." 37 year old, woman

---

"I bless you every day for giving me back my life." 70 year old, woman

---

"I cannot fault this treatment in any way. Without question it saved my life. The kindness and understanding shown with the treatment only added to its effectiveness." 69 year old, man

———————————

"I still let what I learned come to mind and use it to confront my fears. I did not realize I would have a strong physical response when my subconscious mind was responding to the deep truths and events that were so deeply buried within me for years. The truth was potent. The fact that you and Cat gave me permission to release my anger and rage is unforgettable. So cleansing. The energy I released filled the room. The fact that you were with me and talking me through it was so very relieving to me. I felt safe and very comforted by that. The whole process taught me an incredible awareness of all my senses. My connections with others are much, much, stronger. I've learned that I can attend what I want at will. I can relax at will. AWESOME. Thanks." 38 year old, woman

———————————

"It works like a miracle in getting to root of trauma and alleviated pain that was of an emotional nature. It took me several years to find this avenue of relief." 70 year old, woman

———————————

"After being in therapy for many years, I believe this work is a culmination to what I have already learned about myself. It reaches into realms of emotional release that talking can't really touch. It enhances talk therapy in releasing the deeper emotions that need to be expressed in some way. I find it to be exciting and rather awesome in some of the discoveries." 60 year old, woman

---

"I believe in the effectiveness of body oriented psychotherapy 100%. Particularly for clients who have a difficult time accessing their 'stuff.'" 37 year old, man

---

"I am amazed at how quickly we were able to access problem areas, associate present problems to past experiences and eliminate symptoms." 61 year old, woman.

"The body psychotherapy sessions continue to work even six months after treatment. Sometimes the shift in core beliefs do not get tested until long after therapy has ended." 42 year old, woman

---

"I was particularly impressed by the supporting and caring attitude with which you and Cat approached therapy. I feel it was very effective." 58 year old, woman

---

"Thank you Richard and Cat. The work we have done together cannot be measured by numbers or scales. Its effects go deeply and continuously into my soul. Blessings. 39 year old, woman

---

"The warmth and gentle approach of the therapists provide an atmosphere of comfort and trust conductive to creating healing." 67 year old, woman

---

"I feel very fortunate to have experienced this combo gentle touch therapy. It helps target and drain/diffuse areas that have been bottled within my body for over half a century. All these stored emotions (so destructive) kept building and harming my inner spirit hampering me from handling my responses to friends and families and relatives in a controlled and confident manner. I feel released from a bondage." 71 year old, woman

---

"I believe the body therapy combination as well as some medication had profound effects for a year or two following treatment. I'm thrilled that I am no longer depressed at all, after a lifetime of sadness." 70 year old, woman

---

"It is very fast in finding, verifying, treating different issues. It enables the team to confirm the most important issue for the specific treatment and be extremely accurate in the diagnosis. It is by far the best way to go when considering psychotherapy." 32 year old, man

---

"I feel that this is the only way to complete healing. It has benefited me 100%. I also feel it has completed me. Truly, body, mind and soul! The dedication and courage you have in doing this is a great blessing to your patients. Thanks to both of you." 51 year old, woman

---

"It helped." 34 year old, woman

"Keep up the good work. You are both a real gift." 38 year old, man

---

"This therapy allowed me to cut through all the games and insignificant material and get to the core issues. This did not seem possible with conventional methods. It has also answered many questions about my past and why I have reacted the way I have. It has allowed me to put pieces in the puzzle of my life and has introduced me to the concept of choices." 44 year old, woman

---

"The compliment of the male/female energies is wonderful and powerful. It really is a great team." 48 year old, woman

---

"Healing is about forgiveness, both of oneself and of others, and when forgiveness is genuine, everything is different. I suspect I would have eventually come to this same insight without body work therapy, but it would have taken years, and indeed, may not have happened at all." 36 year old, woman

---

"I feel better than ever before, because of everything you taught me." 50 year old, woman

ABOUT THE AUTHOR

Richard G. Schulman, PhD has been a licensed psychologist in the state of Florida since 1987. He has wide experience having worked in many different settings: Adult Inpatient Psychiatric Unit; Adolescent Inpatient Psychiatric Unit; Adolescent Residential Treatment Program; Dual Diagnosis Adolescent Program: Psychosomatic Medicine Unit; Program Coordinator Eating Disorders Program; and Clinical Director of a Chronic Pain Management Unit. He is a former Assistant Professor at the University of South Florida College of Medicine, Department of Psychiatry and Behavioral Medicine.

He received his Doctor of Philosophy degree in Clinical Psychology from the University of South Florida in Tampa. His doctoral dissertation, "Cognitive Distortions in Bulimia," was rewritten as an article and published in the Journal of Personality Assessment. He was a psychology intern at the Palo Alto Veterans Administration Medical Center in Palo Alto, California.

He is a songwriter, having written over 250 songs and is one of the founders of the Dreamwalkers band.

He is a practitioner of Ashtanga Yoga and is currently working with Yogi John McKenney on a book, 'Power Yoga for Aging Athletes." He is the father of two sons; Jonathan, a Licensed Mental Health Counselor, who lives in Boston, Massachusetts, and Daniel, a videographer, living in Sarasota, Florida. He is in private practice in Sarasota, Florida.

Made in the
USA
Columbia, SC